I NEED ANSWER

Yes, Lovey I know you are upset at me for book one. You were not pleased with my cover choice.

As for the content of the book, I know you are upset at me all around but; I refuse to change me to please you. I have to be me whether you like it or not and so far, right now; you do not like me or truly like me, but I truly don't care. Just as how when you are not pleased with me, you unleash all hell on me by stepping aside and letting Death – the evil dead consume me. My life has and have been hell for more than a couple of days now, but it is all good. I am overcoming without your help.

Yes, we both can be petty, and you are pettier than me. That's a fact without doubt. When you are not pleased with me you do step aside thinking I am going to break and come running back to you with my tail between my legs, but I refuse to do so with you. We are both adults and yes, the truth hurt you sometimes but; be God and own up to the truth and not shrug me off by stepping aside from me, and letting hell consume me death wise, and health wise. You are not fair in this way. Nor are you a child. When you do this; let hell be unleashed on me due to your displeasure of me, you're like unto the White Race that refuse to own up to their ills because for them; the White Race, their ills – wrongs here on Earth is correct as well as, their right come on now.

Do not let the truth hurt you. Look into my words. Wrongs can never be right thus, Sin and Hell; Death.

You want and need truth and you have truth in me yet, you want to muzzle me now. Forget it. I refuse to make you muzzle me when it comes to the truth. Like I told you from the get go. I refuse to lie to you in anything I do but; if any in the White Race or any Race for that matter say they own any Waterway of Life, *then we are more than infinitely and indefinitely more than forever ever over.*

Trust me, you have my word of truth that; YOU AS GOD WOULD BE TRULY DEAD TO ME.

I REFUSE YOU IN THIS WAY IF ANYONE SAY THEY OWN ANY WATERWAY IN LIFE HERE ON EARTH, AND IN THE SPIRITUAL REALM BECAUSE; YOU KNOW HOW I TRULY FEEL ABOUT THE WATERWAYS OF LIFE.

THE WATERWAYS OF LIFE BELONG TO ME, YOU, AND OUR GOOD AND TRUE OWN SO TRULY LOOK INTO YOURSELF WITH MOTHER EARTH BECAUSE; YOU MORE THAN TRULY KNOW ME AND MY VENGENCE.

You want to be pissed, be pissed but; *do not be pissed at the truth.* I cannot do to please you day in and day out. The environment of Earth must change for the better good of Good and True Life. And I refuse to go around in circles with you when it comes to Good and True Life.

I refuse to have you abandon Good and True Life. Life is truly not a game so stop treating life as such. Stop hindering Good and True Life here on Earth come on now.

Look at the damage here on Earth. The tone has been set.

The Black Race have and has been through it. Now the Asian Race is facing the same battle we face Racially. NOW TELL ME LOVEY, WHEN IS SLAVERY GOING TO BEGIN FOR THE MONGOLIAN AND OR, ASIAN RACE EXCLUDING BABYLONIAN INDIANS WHO CALL THEMSELVES ASIANS?

When is enough enough with you when it comes to the atrocities and lies of the White Race based on hue and evil deeds?

I've had enough, and I am having enough of you too Lovey because; You, and Mother Earth are truly not fair and just in my book right now.

Yes, you maybe upset at me, but I have to be frank and speak my mind with you whether you like it or not.

Life is a given yes, but life should not come down to the evil games or any game or games that humans play. My life is worth it therefore, I have to cherish life.

Life should not come down to the game of WHO LIVES AND WHO DIES WHEN IT COMES TO THE WHITE RACE OR ANY RACE FOR THAT MATTER. Yes, you can say, well what about what you write in separating good from evil, and letting Death go with their wicked and evil own?

I have a right to say that Lovey because in your realm; GOOD IS SEPARATATED FROM ALL EVIL. NO EVIL CAN COME INTO YOUR ABODE BECAUSE DEATH HAS AND HAVE MADE IT SO.

YOUR ABODE IS CLEAN AND DEATH FREE, so why can't I have this goodness here on Earth for the good and true including, myself?

Yes, billions have and has chosen Death for self, but how did they choose Lovey?

How did many choose Death?

WAS LIFE GIVEN OR TRULY GIVEN?

Is it not Death that is given, and truly given here on Earth for Life?

So now tell me Lovey, *how can anyone escape Death if all we are given to live by is Death?*

How can we look to you for hope, life, strength, morals, moral values, good life values if; all we are given, and all we know is Death Lovey?

So, when I come at you hard for answers, do not be ashamed, or block me from your window, door, home,

4

thoughts, your world and kingdom, and more. You tell me when I am wrong.

You tell me when I am doing wrong, so why can't I with you in this way?

You've never barred me before. So, why now that I have displeased you with the cover on book one, and with my line and tone about the waterways in my book *THE MIND AND SPIRITUALITY.*

Extremely candid and exact I am with you yet, you cannot be the same with me; why?

Why does everything have to come down to begging, and fighting with you when it comes to me?

Why do I continually have to beg you for all that is right and just; true?

Why do I have to beg you for life here on Earth?

As humans we do wrongs yes, but; *THE GOOD SHOULD NOT HAVE TO SUFFER FOR THE BAD AS WELL AS, DIE WITH THE BAD COME ON NOW.*

How the hell would you feel if; *EVIL – THE WICKED AND EVIL OF EARTH WAS IN YOUR HOME – REALM?*

HOW WOULD YOU LOVEY FEEL IF EVIL – THE WICKED AND EVIL WAS IN YOUR REALM DESTROYING IT?

You have done all to separate yourself from all that is wicked and evil in the Spiritual Realm – Your World Lovey. *So, why can't you do this – Let Mother Earth separate all who are good from all who are evil in her?*

You Lovey of yourself could not live with any form of evil. I know this for a fact without doubt. You as Lovey and God would have created a different space for yourself farther than you are now. Just as man – anyone unclean cannot get into your domain now, we would never be able to get into your new domain if you created one if; the wicked and evil got access to your world, and domain right now. So now tell me, what is so different between me and you when it comes to cleanliness of all for me, you, and our good and true own here on Earth?

What are you telling me Lovey?

Are you telling me our lives matter not to you here on Earth?

Are you truly telling me, our well being and sanity here on Earth matters not to you?

Are you truly telling me, our health and truth including, spiritual well being matters not to you?

Earth need positive life changes Lovey come on now.

You and Mother Earth need to do something for the better good of Earth and the good and true of Earth come on now. Life isn't a joke therefore, You and Mother Earth should not treat life as a joke come on now.

Yes, I might be unfair to you because you did give us people to teach – educate us.

Bob Marley – You gave him songs to educate the Black Race.

Marcus Mosiah Garvey – You gave enterprise to educate the Black Race.

Me – You gave wisdom, knowledge, vision, words, these books despite the many grammatical errors people will encounter to educate the Black Race by.

But Lovey, it's hard for me. How many have I sent books to, and is truly ignored?

Yes, I am impersonal. I like staying in the shadows. Marketing the conventional way is truly not me. Thus, all of you who is/are reading this book. Please help me to spread the Message of Truth no matter how doubtful you are of me. Truly help me to save you by letting some of my goodness and mercy fall on you and truly save you. Truly help me in a good and true way to promote these books.

Onwards I go. Life is not Death therefore, you Lovey and Mother Earth should not treat life as such; Death.

Life is Life, and Death is Death. What part of this do You and Mother Earth not comprehend?

When you keep Life – the good and true around those who are not of Life, we do take on the Sin and Sins of those who are not of Life. Now tell me, how fair is that to us who are trying to live life clean, good, honest, and true; pure?

How can you say you are God and *"LOVE US SO,"* quoting you Lovey, *and you keep us in unclean environments that isn't even suitable for you?*

You of yourself cannot go into unclean environments so, why are you keeping your seeds; the good and true in unclean environments they don't want or need to be in?

When you do this Lovey, keep us in environments that is not even suitable for you, *ARE YOU NOT CAUSING US TO SIN AGAINST YOU, AND ALL THAT IS CLEAN, GOOD, AND TRUE?*

Are you not contributing to our downfall in this way here on Earth?

Are you Lovey not keeping us in hell in this way here on Earth?

So tell me, *HOW GOOD AND TRUE ARE YOU TO LIFE – ALL THAT IS GOOD AND TRUE; CLEAN AND TRULY CLEAN?*

Now tell me, *HOW CAN I NOT BLAME YOU FOR KEEPING ME, AS WELL AS, THE GOOD AND*

TRUE OF LIFE AMONGST THE CHILDREN AND PEOPLE OF DEATH – EVIL?

The Sins of man affect us all Lovey, so how can anyone here on Earth say they are clean when; YOU LOVEY AND MOTHER EARTH ALLOW ATROCITIES TO HAPPEN HERE ON EARTH?

How can I not blame you Lovey because you cannot truly love? You can only *"SO LOVE AND OR, LOVE SO."*

How can I not blame you Lovey when You and Mother Earth cannot provide a good, clean, and true environment for the Children and People of Life to live in good and true; clean?

How can we not blame you Lovey and Mother Earth for pushing the Children and People of Life over the edge?

You open the Realm of Death to us; well, me, and you know how debilitating Hell and Death is for me yet, on some days you let Death consume me. The Valley of Death is truly not for me, so why allow Earth to become the *TRUE VALLEY OF DEATH – PHYSICAL DEATH?*

Meaning, why open up the Foundation of Life here on Earth to Death?

Your realm Death cannot come in; enter. So, why let Death come into Earth?

Yes, I know the *CHOICE OF HUMANS.* But Lovey, those who need a good, true, and clean life with you.

Separate us here on Earth from those who do not need a good, true, and clean life from you, or with you.

In separating us from those who do not require a good, true, and clean life from you Lovey, ensure these people cannot come into our space or lands. Just as you have set up impenetrable frameworks, and foundations in the Spiritual Realm for You and Your People. Do the same here on Earth for our good and true people come on now.

Now answer me this Lovey. Why allow Death to infiltrate Earth this way; Death Wise?

Why could you not protect Earth from Death Lovey?

Is this not the same with me here on Earth?

Yes, you protect yet; you cannot fully and truly protect me from Death – the evil dead; why?

Why are you powerless against Death here on Earth in this way Lovey?

Can You Lovey change for the better good?

Meaning, can you change the environment of Earth to be truly good and true; clean?

What is it about me that I cannot fully get You Lovey to come my way when it comes to my truth, thinking, goodness, cleanliness, good and true life, happiness, moral values, morals, and more?

You know what, let me leave it alone because; I've just lost my train of thought. But Lovey, *why isn't life important to you here on Earth?*

If you truly love us, or love us so, why do you continually let evil destroy the good and true of Earth?

Why are you sacrificing us; the Good and True to Death in this way?

Lovey, *THE CHOICE.*

Now let me ask you this. Why keep your Children and People which is our Children and People amongst the unclean here on Earth?

Meaning, Babylon is Death we know this for a fact without doubt. Therefore, the Cow, and Rolling Cow that comes with Fire – Death.

The White Race have and has chosen Death for self therefore, their lies, religious lies, scientific lies, medical lies, political lies, judicial lies, universal lies – lies told on space, educational lies, penitentiaries of death, pharmaceuticals of death, wars – armies of death, war machines, viruses, different diseases; all that they devise and manufacture to eliminate all life including the life of Earth. Now tell me Lovey, *why keep the different races in one domain?*

The different races are not in one domain in the Spiritual Realm from what I gather. So, why keep the different races in one domain – here on Earth?

Babylon and the White Race chose Death for self, why not separate them; these races from the Black and Asian; Mongolian Race?

I've made my choice for good and true life for the good and true seeds you've given me to plant. So, why are You Lovey not separating *OUR SEED FROM THE DEVIL'S*

11

SEED, THE CHILDREN AND PEOPLE OF BABYLON, AND SEEDS OF DEATH AND DESTRUCTION; THE WHITE RACE?

Separate Good and True Life from Death now. Do not wait until the Mongolian Race have and has made their decision for Life, or Death.

Now, did you truly think of my choice of goodness and truth?

No Lovey, I have to ask because; I thought things would have been set up long ago that when I made the choice to continue with good and true life – You, you would have set the separation up of Good and Evil in this way to be automatic. Earth would separate to keep evil out of the domains of good.

In your domain Lovey, Life cannot bow down to Death. So, why do you continue to let this happen here on Earth?

Meaning, why do you continue to let your; our good and true Children and People bow down to death?

Lovey, Earth is run by the Wicked and Evil therefore, we as your good and true own should not look to or go to Evil for bread – food.

We/I am /are looking to you Lovey to keep us, and feed us right and true, and you are disappointing us; the good and true Life Wise here on Earth. Why?

Lovey, when we live amongst the Children and People of Death are we not bowing down to Death?

Think Lovey.

You cannot say you *"LOVE US SO,"* and keep us as the sacrificial lambs unto Death come on now. My life with you should not come down to me losing my life to Death to get to you because; *no one can get to you in Death* and you, and I know this. So now tell me, *WHERE DO WE GO FROM HERE WITH OUR TRUTH* because; I am doubting your truth for me and good and true life?

Yes, I am listening to *Jodeci's song CRY FOR YOU.*

Now let me ask you this Lovey; do you even cry for your; our good and true Children and People?

Are you even capable of shedding tears for us?

Are we your everything in life?

If we are, *WHY IS IT THAT YOU ARE NOT DOING EVERYTHING FOR US IN GOODNESS AND TRUTH IN LIFE HERE ON EARTH?*

WHY IS IT THAT YOU ARE KEEPING US AMONGST THE LIVING AND WALKING DEAD – DEATH'S CHILDREN AND PEOPLE?

Why is it that you cannot partition Earth, and separate all who are good from all facets of wickedness and evil?

Now tell me Lovey. If you were for us; the good and true; why are we not moving towards you good and true?

Why is it that you are not giving us the path and pathway to walk good and true; truly clean back to you?

Why do we have to bug you so much; well, me. Why do I have to bug you so much for the *TRUTH OF LIFE FOR OUR GOOD AND TRUE OWN?*

No Lovey. *WHY LEAVE OUT OF EARTH IF YOU TRULY DID NOT WANT TO LEAVE?*

WHY LET US GO IF YOU TRULY DID NOT WANT TO LET US GO?

WHY WANT US BACK AFTER DIVORCING US, AND MOTHER EARTH?

YOU SHOULD HAVE KEPT US IF YOU DID NOT WANT TO LET US GO.

Now that I am talking to you, *YOU ARE REFUSING TO DO ALL TO SEPARATE GOOD – ALL GOOD FROM ALL EVIL HERE ON EARTH; WHY?*

No, I will not go down on my knees to pray to you and for you because right now Lovey, you truly do not make any sense to me with your thinking and truth. Because in full and true truth, I don't think your truth is true or truly true.

Yes, I see things but; I cannot live or continue to live in your lies. The power is there to change this world; Earth yet, you refuse to allow change in this way; why?

Yes, the Physical and Spiritual. But Lovey, is not the Physical and Spiritual joined in flesh?

Are we as humans not Physical and Spiritual?

So where does the problem lie with you?

You cannot be our Kiss of Death Lovey come on now.
You cannot be our Hope then just hand us over to Death.
You cannot be my Truth then turn around and laugh at us; me.

Look at the Lockdown here on Ontario. The Premier LOCKING DOWN ONTARIO ON APRIL 1st, THUS CALLING US THE FOOL. WE THE PEOPLE OF ONTARIO WERE, AND ARE HIS APRIL FOOLS JOKE. Because that is what he is telling us. He is telling us we are the fool and fools.

So now tell me Lovey, how can anyone have compassion for the White Race of Demons that LIVE TO HURT PEOPLE INTENTIONALLY?

No. You locking them; THE WHITE RACE OUT OF YOUR KINGDOM AND DOMAIN DO NOT BRING ME JOY OR PLEASURE INCLUDING, HOPE HERE ON EARTH. I WANT AND NEED THEM ALL GONE FROM EARTH PERIOD.

You cannot live to kill and do kill and expect me to be pleased with your race.

LIES ARE NOT TRUTHS LOVEY COME ON NOW.

So no, I am truly not happy with you because this DEMONIC RACE HAVE CONTROL OF EARTH, AND RULE EARTH IN LIES AND DECEIT. And with you Lovey, the truth is not forthcoming. Meaning, those who like me that want truth in life cannot separate from this race period. I've asked you, when is enough enough with you Lovey and this, you can't even tell me.

Yes, you've shown me a world without White People, but I cannot wait for this to happen. I need true justice here on Earth.

I need truth to be separated from lies come on now.
I can't beg you anymore for the *TRUTH OF LIFE* anymore Lovey because to me, you are truly not true to Life; any life.

You cannot give me hope via my dream world to just shatter me to pieces in this way come on now. When did I become a joke to you?

When did I become your joke Physically and Spiritually Lovey?

When did I become your true fool?

The fool that trust you with all only to have you break my heart, my true heart, my truth, true love; all of me.

Do you even give a damn about me and all that you have given me?

Do not claim and or say, You *"LOVE SO AND OR, SO LOVE US,"* and show me the magnitude of *"LOVE SO"* to shatter me into pieces.

How much more should I show you and teach you?
How much more should I write to you and for you?
How much more hell should rain down on me?

How much more hell should I go through before you say, that's it; let me do the good and true that Michelle and our good and true seeds; people need from me?

How much more tears should be shed before my tears and the tears of the good and true reach you Lovey?

Why open your door to me only to slam your door shut in my face?

You cannot divorce us here on Earth only to want and need some of us back. It makes no sense come on now.

How much more disappointment should I face with you and from you Lovey?

I've put all my trust and truth in you for you to BREAK ME DOWN IN EVERY WAY LOVEY; WHY?

Why break me down like this man come on now?

Why break me Lovey?
Why break me?

Lovey, hear me now and see what I am trying to say with you here on Earth because; I am on Earth, and not in the Spiritual Realm with you. *LOCKING THE WHITE RACE OUT OF YOUR KINGDOM AND ABODE IN THE SPIRITUAL REALM IS TRULY NOT THE SAME AS LOCKING THE WHITE RACE OUT OF THE PHYSICAL REALM.*

Look

Am I not in the same land and abode as the White Race?

Is this race – the White Race and Babylonian Race not on Earth with me?

So now tell me, *how is that locking the White Race out of Life here on Earth.*

You cannot just lock a race and people out of the Spiritual Realm without locking them out of the Physical Realm also.

When you do this; lock a race out of the Spiritual Realm only, you are like unto man and the way man – humans divorce each other.

Divorce cannot be ½ way. Divorce and Locking Out have to be full way come on now.

<u>*When humans divorce ½ way; they are sinning as well as, living in adulterous relationships if they take on another partner.*</u> They are not fully divorced, and you know this Lovey. So, why leave the good and true here on Earth in environments that cause us to Sin as well as, take on more sin thus, adding more time to the Life of Death, and the Demons of Hell?

You've guaranteed the safety of the Spiritual Realm when it comes to evil yet, you cannot guarantee the safety of the Physical Realm when it comes to all facets of evil, and wickedness and evil; why?

<u>*So now tell me. How can you guarantee Life if the life of the good and true here on Earth you cannot guarantee?*</u>

And the reason why I say this is because evil – the evil dead do find me.

Death do wreak havoc on my physical and spiritual well being here on Earth. So, what say you in this way Lovey?

Am I the only one that goes though this torment Lovey because; I choose and chose *GOOD AND TRUE LIFE OVER DEATH?*

So yes Lovey, I have a lot of questions when it comes to you.

I shouldn't have to validate you if that makes any sense.

I shouldn't have to do so much for you to comprehend what I am trying to say to you honestly and truthfully.

No Lovey, it's not a competition between you and me.

As God, you should see and know and make the necessary changes before hand when it comes to the good and true of life.

How much more should I write and say to prove my truth and true worth to you?

How much more should I write and say to prove that the good and true of life here on Earth need positive changes for them in an environment that they do not have to worry about the Evil Beings of this world – those who did not choose good and true life for self and family?

How much more should I write and go through for you Lovey and the good and true of life?

Saving us Spiritually is great and I truly thank you for this but, *how about saving us Physically as well?*

Does our Physical Well Being not matter to you?

I don't know but I am starving for life spiritually and physically here on Earth, and you Lovey and Mother Earth cannot see this. Why the true separation Lovey if this could have been prevented from the beginning?

Why show me such power yet, this power cannot be used here on Earth?

No one here on Earth have used this power in my view. Yes, I could be wrong given Earth and the nature of Earth, but why show me things yet, things cannot change for the better good here on Earth in my view?

What is the difference between You and Mother Earth Lovey?

What is the difference between the Physical and Spiritual?

Yes, there is truly something I am missing thus, the question of difference. Why death here on Earth?

Why do people live for Death instead of living for Life?

Why couldn't the Physical and Spiritual be truly clean here on Earth?

Why Physical and Spiritual Death in this way?
Why separate the two if both were once joined?

Yes, I know creation and pro-creation, but I am truly missing something all around to do with Life and Death. I do not know the full history and or, beginning of Life and Death.

There has to be more and there is more because nothing is balanced here on Earth and in the Universe. Yes, things are balanced with you because your realm is clean, but in all other realms especially here on Earth things are truly not balanced because; *EVIL DID INTEGRATE WITH GOOD.*

GOOD DID MARRY EVIL, AND EVIL DID MARRY GOOD.

The two could not be separated in this way and I cannot comprehend why. Maybe things go back to Creation and Procreation, but I am truly missing something, and you Lovey are/is not showing me the fullness of what I need to know when it comes to You, Life, Mother Earth, the

Spiritual Realm, the good and true seeds you given me, and more. I truly hate being limited with you Lovey and I am. What I need to know you are not showing me or teaching me fully.

Why give me seeds if I cannot receive these seeds here on Earth?

Why give me seeds that I cannot fully and truly use; plant good and true here on Earth?

I need to know the true beginning and why you are separated from Earth.

Why did you not put up impenetrable foundations and frameworks here on Earth so that Evil could not infiltrate the Garden of Eden – Mother Earth – *Woman?*

Why did Mother Earth have to sacrifice herself for Good and Evil in that way?

Why did she have to give a home to all facets of evil in her in that way?

Lovey, did Mother Earth have a choice?

Did Mother Earth choose, and chose Evil – Death for Self?

No, I truly don't think Mother Earth chose, and choose Death for Self in that way.

Maybe this is beyond me and you truly don't want and need me to know these things Lovey but, something is truly not right everywhere in my view. What I seek to know and need to know you are keeping from me; why?

Knowledge is one of the keys to Life Lovey and if I have not knowledge, how am I to know?

If you keep your door and doors closed to me, how can I open them and or, your door and come in if I do not know the truth?

I need to cleanse my spiritual self Lovey, and if I cannot clean my spiritual self; how can I receive you, or come clean and true to you?

If my thoughts are scattered; all over the place and impure Lovey, how can I come good and true; fully clean to you?

You say, yet; you keep me and others away; why?

You say, yet; you cannot give so that we can get, and come to you clean and whole the way we are; why?

I cannot battle you anymore for the truth Lovey come on now.

I need to and have to take time for me, because in many ways you are closed to me. Your door is so closed that I cannot open you anymore and this is truly sad in my view. You want and need me to be true to you yet, *YOU RAPE ME OF THE KNOWLEDGE AND TRUTH I SEEK WHEN IT COMES TO LIFE AND YOU; why?*

The Foundation of Life should not be about lies and or, secrets come on now. So, why are you so secretive when it comes to me?

Do you feel I want to outdo you?
Do you feel insecure when it comes to me?

Do you feel as if I am not trustworthy?

If so, why be around me?
Why show me things?
Why reveal certain things to me?

Aye Lovey, I truly don't know with you anymore because the life I need for us, is truly not the life you want or need for us in my view. Shameful yes, but it's life with You I guess. *Nothing is truly for sure with you given your nature of INSECURITY.*

You've been hurt and I've been hurt too. It is you now that need to let go of the baggage that hinder you in life when it comes to me and you, Mother Earth, and Life Wise. You cannot go on not trusting me or others. You need to put yourself together and truly live truthfully now come on now.

Life is truly not a game thus, *SINS ARE REAL.* Sins impact our life here on Earth and in the Spiritual Realm come on now.

Now I ask you Lovey. When is enough enough with the White Race of Vipers when it comes to you and me, and them being here on Earth?

Why do they have to enslave people and take our Basic Fundamental Human Rights from us here on Earth?

No Lovey. I am fed up of the bullshit they put us through. Look at the way they've treated Black People based on hue. Have they not taken our rights from us?

Look at South Africa and the evils they've done in that land to Black People?

Look at Slavery and the evils they've done to Black People?

Why is it that with all the atrocities this plagued race has and have done to Blacks here on Earth, You continue to let this evil race succeed; do all manner of ills here on Earth, and let them get away with it?

Do you even care Lovey?

Do you even have your morals and moral values intact because; I truly do not think so with all the evils You, and Mother Earth let happen here on Earth?

This race – the White Race is cut off from you in your world; realm. Why can't this be done here on Earth; the White Race being cut off fully and truly from all who are good and true, and of life?

What is wrong with You and Mother Earth Lovey?

Why is truth and goodness so hard for the both of you?

You cannot want and need life for people and keep them trapped in societies controlled by demons – the wicked and evil come on now. What the hell kind of life is that?

Are we not like caged animals right now given the situation of Earth with the different diseases and viruses humans create?

Lovey, you showed me the White Race being the Sick/Sikh Race. Why have them amongst us here on Earth?

Why continue to have them on Your Mountain – the Mountain of Life?

Why have them control Earth?

What is it about this lying and deceiving race that pleases you?

What is it about life that You Lovey hate that you have to let the White Race have total and absolute control of Earth, and the People of Earth?

Do you like slavery?

Is that why you blatantly allow this race – the White Race to get away with all their ills here on Earth?

The lie went as far as Life – You Lovey, and you've done absolutely nothing to help yourself by vindicating you, and cutting off all access to life here on Earth to the White Race; why?

What does Death have over You and Mother Earth that the both of you; You and Mother Earth have to bow down to Death, and the Will of Death and their people?

Yes, I am mad because I want and need to travel, and I cannot travel the normal means nor; are you showing me, and giving me another way to travel Lovey. So therefore, You Lovey is keeping me Shackled and Chain to the White Man's Way. Now tell me, how fair is that to me; anyone who refuse the White Way of Life?

WHY THE HELL SHOULD ANYONE LIVE WHITE?

Isn't the White way – White Man's Way Death Lovey?

*So, why should anyone live the White Way;
Death's Way?*

*Why the hell should I give up my Blackness for
Whiteness?*

No Lovey, truly do not let me get more angry because; I am angry right now.

Where is Justice for the Just here on Earth?

What say do we have here on Earth when it comes to Life?

Why should the Wicked and Evil control it all?

Where is life for me here on Earth?

No, I am tired of waiting on you; a God that truly do not give a damn about my living and living situation here on Earth. Why are you keeping me trapped in an environment that I truly do not want or need to be in?

No Lovey, it's best if we separated permanently because you are truly not good for me Life Wise, Health Wise, Financially, Land Wise, Water Wise, and more here on Earth.

No, you are not truly good for me all around. I cannot keep bugging you for Justice and you are turning you back to me.

I can't keep begging you to separate the Good and True from Evil Beings – the Wicked and Evil of this Earth. All I do is ask in vain because you like Slavery in my view.

You like to see others hurting your people.

You like to see us suffer.

You like to see us in pain, health wise, financially, home wise, land wise, emotionally, you Lovey Wise, food wise, water wise, Death Wise, and more. Therefore, I should have known that you Lovey cannot be truly true to anyone thus; "YOUR LOVE SO."

You are not the truth because; the TRUTH CANNOT LIE. NOR IS THE TRUTH UNJUST IN ANY WAY.

You cannot see the demise of TRUTH HERE ON EARTH AND NOT PROVIDE A TRUE SANCTUARY FOR OUR PEOPLE; THE GOOD AND TRUE OF LIFE.

So yes, I am the true fool for trusting in you and putting all my trust and hope in you for a better life, a better Earth, better all around. Thus, you Lovey are, and is *MY HURT AND SHAME. We as Black People are the gullible ones THAT HAS AND HAVE PUT THEIR/OUR TRUTH AND TRUST IN LIARS THAT DECEIVE AND KILL THEM; US. Thus, you're no different Lovey because; "Loving us so" is truly not loving us true.*

Yes, this is the way I feel right now due to my anger, and I refuse to take my anger back. I refuse to lie to you in the way I feel.

Why deceive me so man come on now?

Why do to me like he did to me?
Why become him in every sense of the way?
Why abuse and betray me and my trust like that?

Does truth not matter to you?
Are you even capable of truth?
Are you capable of Life?

What is your worth in Life Lovey?

What is your true worth in Life if you as God cannot honour your word to me?

Yes, you can be angry at me, but I am angry at you. My life hath worth, and I should not live my life in vain because of you and the White Race come on now.

My Life hath Value; Worth so, why are you allowing *DEMONS TO TAKE MY LIFE'S WORTH FROM ME AND OTHERS INCLUDING, YOU?*

ABSOLUTELY NO ONE CAN HAVE TRUTH LIVING IN LIES LOVEY COME ON NOW.

How the hell can anyone attain you if all we are given is/are lies?

Now tell me God and Lovey. *WHAT IS UNITY TO YOU?*

Can you truly unite with anyone here on Earth for the better good of the good and true here on Earth?

Now tell me. Why are you not attainable here on Earth?

Why is everything so difficult with you?
Why are you limited here on Earth?

Why is it that many of my asking go unanswered?

Why is it that you are failing me?

Why is it that You and Earth are truly separated a part from, cleanliness; humans making Earth the Valley of Death – Physical Death?

Your domain is safe and secure in the Spiritual Realm for the good and true Lovey, but why is Earth not secure and safe for the good and true, and truly trying to be good?

Why is it that we – the good and true and truly trying to be good is blacklisted from Life; You Lovey?

No one can succeed in life if all they are given is failure.

No one can succeed in life if they are not given the right tools to succeed, and you know this Lovey come on now. So, why are you giving me failure?

Why do you truly want me to fail in life?

Knowledge is one of the keys to life, and if we have not knowledge; how can we know?

How will we learn?

I know you are not for all but really with the lack of knowledge Lovey!!!!

And no, I will not make excuses for you this time around. And don't you dare bring your timeline into this.

Speed
Vibration
Communication - Language

Velocity without the change in time because; Time cannot change. *Time is Constant.*

Speed changes therefore the Rate of Speed but, *Time cannot change* this I know for a fact without doubt. Yes, there Physical Time and Spiritual Time, but Time is Time. Time cannot change to please or suit anyone. Time must be constant therefore, *absolutely no one can speed up Time or stop Time or even measure time.*

If man could change Time, they could, and would be able to change the TIME OF THEIR DEATH. Plus, if man could change Time, they would not die, nor would there be Death. Death would cease to exist all around.

Yes Lovey. I need the true formulas to Life in relation to Physical Time, Gravity, Speed, Spiritual Time, Vibration, Creation, Space, and more.

You know what. Let me stop there because the SCIENCE OF MAN IS TRULY NOT THE SCIENCE OF GOD – YOU LOVEY.

I so do not know why you Lovey allow Lies to take precedence over Truth.

I truly do not know why you continue to allow Good to live amongst Evil.

I truly do not know why You and Mother Earth do not separate Good from Evil here on Earth.

I truly do not know why Life here on Earth with You Lovey have to be so damned complicated that it frustrates the heck and hell out of me.

I truly do not know why you do certain things to get me mad; angry at you in so many ways. Look at Life Lovey come on now. When I say I want to do something that you do not approve of, look how quick you caution me on my life with you spiritually, yet, SEPARATING GOOD FROM ALL EVIL HERE ON EARTH IS IMPOSSIBLE FOR YOU: WHY?

And I am going to insert RIDE NATTY RIDE by Bob Marley and the Wailers.

Yes, I know:

"EARTH IS GOING TO BURN."

Now tell me Lovey. WHAT GROUNDS DO MOTHER EARTH HAVE FOR NOT WANTING TO SEPARATE GOOD FROM EVIL?

WHAT IS THE FUNDAMENTAL OF LIFE FOR MOTHER EARTH?

WHAT DISAGREEMENT DO YOU AND MOTHER EARTH HAVE THAT THE PHYSICAL AND SPIRITUAL IS SEPARATED IN THAT WAY?

Lovey, look at the ills from the past until now of the White Race and tell me, *WHY DO THEY GET AWAY WITH THEIR ILLS HERE ON EARTH?*

WHY DO THEY HAVE FULL DOMINION HERE ON EARTH?

WHY DO THEY HAVE FULL DOMINION OF EARTH?

WHY CAN'T THIS RACE BE STOPPED HERE ON EARTH?

WHY DO THEY FEEL AS IF THEY OWN EARTH AND EVERYTHING ON EARTH?

Lovey, look at what the Dutch – White Race has and have done to South Africa and MANY AFRICAN LANDS and tell me, if all the ills they've done in the name of DESTRUCTION, GREED, COLONIZATION, ERADICATING A RACE OF PEOPLE, AND DEATH JUSTIFIED?

Lovey, look at what the French – White Race has and have done to MANY AFRICAN LANDS and tell me, if all the ills the French have and has done to Black Africans in the name of DESTRUCTION, GREED, COLONIZATION, ERADICATING A RACE OF PEOPLE, AND DEATH JUSTIFIED?

Lovey, look at what the English – England – White Race has and have done to MANY AFRICAN LANDS AND CARIBBEAN LANDS and tell me, if all the ills the English – England have and has done to Black Africans and Blacks of the Caribbean in the name of DESTRUCTION, COLONIZATION, ERADICATING A RACE OF PEOPLE, AND DEATH JUSTIFIED?

As Blacks, _we cannot get away with our ills_ yet, BABYLON AND THE WHITE RACE HAVE AND HAS GOTTEN AWAY WITH THEIR ILLS HERE ON EARTH; WHY?

WHY IS IT JUSTIFIED FOR THE WHITE RACE AND BABYLON TO USE BLACK PEOPLE AS THEIR HANG MAN AND GET AWAY WITH MURDER?

Blacks have and has been lynched by all why?

Do we have no rights here on Earth?

What is so bad about being Black that every race want(s) to eradicate us?

Yes, I know we are a SPECIAL RACE OF PEOPLE but Lovey; WHY PUT US IN THE LINE OF FIRE AMONGST THE HEATHENS OF LIFE?

Segregation
Segregation
Segregation

WHY ALLOW GOOD TO BE INTEGRATED WITH EVIL WHEN YOU KNOW HOW DEADLY AND DESTRUCTIVE EVIL IS?

EVIL CANNOT BE CLEAN NOR CAN EVIL LIVE CLEAN.

EVIL HAVE TO KILL BECAUSE THE JOB OF EVIL IS TO DESTROY AND KILL BY ANY MEANS NECESSARY. YOU KNOW THIS LOVEY YET, YOU KEEP OUR GOOD AND TRUE PEOPLE IN HARMS WAY HERE ON EARTH; WHY?

EVIL CANNOT BE REFORMED NOR DOES EVIL WANT TO BE REFORMED COME ON NOW.

It's time to chase those Demonic; Wicked and Evil baldheads out of Earth more than infinitely and indefinitely more than continually without end.

CRAZY BALDHEADS – Bob Marley.

You cannot say; *"YOU LOVE SO,"* and let your people which is our good and true people die at the hands of the wicked and evil come on now.

Right now, we are in what I call "GLOBAL SLAVERY" with Covid-19 yet, the White Leaders of the Globe including their diseased scientists that create diseases and viruses get away with murder; all the wrongs they are doing to Nations. Now tell me Lovey, if that was us in the Black Race doing such shit would you not let us get caught, thrown in jail, whooped by you, and more?

No, don't because you would let it happen Spiritually and Physically to us; the good and true because; *I AM A LIVING TESTAMENT OF THIS,* and you cannot deny this fact come on now.

Therefore, I ask You Lovey and Mother Earth this.

"WHAT MAKES THE WHITE RACE SO SPECIAL THAT THEY CAN GET AWAY WITH MURDER – GENOCIDE HERE ON EARTH, AND NOT BE PUNISHED SEVERELY HERE ON EARTH?"

Was not Black People enslaved and many eradicated by the White Race of Demons?

So, what makes their actions different from the past until now including tomorrow?

WHEN DID TRUE LIFE BECOME EVIL LOVEY FOR YOU AND MOTHER EARTH THAT HUMANS CAN ERADICATE AT WILL HERE ON EARTH AND YOU AND MOTHER EARTH JUST STAND ASIDE AND LOOK?

PROPAGANDA – Lutan Fyah

Now tell me Lovey, WHY IS IT THAT BLACK LIVES MATTERS NOT FOR THE DIFFERENT RACES?

WHY IS IT THAT THE DEVIL'S CHILDREN – THE CHILDREN AND PEOPLE OF DEMONS – THE WHITE RACE ARE LEFT HERE ON EARTH TO KILL – ERADICATE ALL WHO OPPOSE THEM AND THE ILLS THEY DO TO THE DIFFERENT NATIONS ESPECIALLY THE BLACK NATIONS, AND TRUE BLACK NATIONS?

Now tell me Lovey; Why do Black People have to struggle so much here on Earth after all we've done to establish civilization globally?

Why is it that the different races are threatened by us and our knowledge that they have to water down, and whitewash all that we've done; created?

Why do we as Blacks go hungry and cry out to you Lovey for everything and you just leave us begging as if we truly do not matter at all?

Now look at the Black Race Globally and what we have become here on Earth.

We've become so accepting of wrongs that we as Black People has and have forgotten about you and the law and laws you've set up for us to live by. So now tell me, how can anyone attain you when; *OUR CULTURE, THOUGHTS, GOD, ENVIRONMENT, VALUES, MORAL VALUES, LAW AND LAWS, US AS PEOPLE HAVE AND HAS CHANGED FOR THE NEGATIVE NOT THE POSITIVE?*

Why do we have to fight for our rights here on Earth Lovey?

Why allow Evil access to Earth all around?

Why did Mother Earth allow Evil access to Earth all around Lovey?

Look at the Blood that is being spilt on land.
Look at the Death toll that is here on Earth.
Look at the Crimes that plague Earth.

Look how humans are taught to hate each other.

Look at the different hate crimes globally.

Now tell me, *is racial indifference; prejudice worth it?*

We are not experiments, or test subjects. No, let me take that back because; billions are experiments; test subjects for White People – the White Race because they do all manner of evil scientifically, religiously, sexually, hate wise, economy wise, family wise, psychologically, socially, earth wise, life wise, and get away with it here on Earth because they write the Laws of Men; their unjust laws to cripple nations. Cause Nations to bow down to their evil and disgusting will. Therefore Lovey, the Laws of Men especially the White Man's Laws cannot be just. They; their laws will forever ever be unjust because they write LAWS TO PLEASE THEM, HONOUR THEM, GET OTHERS TO BOW DOWN TO THEM AND THEIR ILL WILL, AND MORE. THUS, THEIR NASTY BOOK – SO-CALLED HOLY BIBLE THAT THEY TEACH HATE, STRIFE, ALL AROUND LIES, DEATH, AND DECEIT, ADULTERY, THEFT, MURDER, AND MORE FROM.

So no Lovey, LIFE CANNOT BE FAIR AND JUST HERE ON EARTH BECAUSE IT'S THE UNJUST THAT HATH POWER, AND IS USING THIS POWER TO DOMINATE AND CONTROL OTHERS ACCORDING TO THEIR ILL AND DEMENTED ILL WILLS – MURDER.

Murder is murder Lovey therefore, I will forever advocate and complain to you about this Sick/Sikh Race of Demons that plague the life of humans here on Earth with their destructive and murderous ways. Ways you Lovey and Mother Earth refuse to shut down here on Earth.

Therefore, I still cannot comprehend fully why You and Mother Earth is separated in that way.

Now for my dreams this Morning April 15, 2021. Dreamt I was standing by this Brick Wall, and others was/were outside. We were not wearing masks, nor were we social distancing. My back was to the Brick Wall and this White Man came up to us and said something about the law, and that I could not stand there by the wall. It was illegal. Something to that effect anyway. I had to put him in his place and tell him *"why doesn't his race stop making viruses?"* He got offended and said, *"his race do not do that"* then fled. *In the dream, he knew the truth that his race – the White Race created this virus, but had to save face by lying.* After that you saw Asians gathering because; the crowd I was amongst was mainly Asians that looked more Japanese, and we began to party; have fun dancing.

So yes, *THE WHITE RACE AND OR, THERE ARE PEOPLE OUT THERE THAT KNOW THE TRUTH, AND REFUSE TO TELL/SPEAK THE TRUTH ABOUT THE DIFFERENT VIRUSES*

THAT ARE DESIGNED AND MANUFACTURED IN LABS TO KILL SO THAT THE PHARMACEUTICAL DISGUSTS OF THE WORLD CAN USE THE CITIZENS OF THE GLOBE AS THEIR TEST SUBJECTS FOR THEIR EVIL.

In the dream I believe I brought that up too. When I was defending me with the White Guy. See in the dream, *I was a threat.* Thus, after that dream, I dreamt not crow, but I would say a Vulture but not exactly a Vulture watching me as I walked in this underground garage. I will not analyze the bird part of the dream. It is what it is because many will not like what I write in these books.

Many will think me to be racist and more but, *I truly do not care.* Earth do not have to be this way with humans hating and killing each other. The way Earth is with the different ills is not apart of God's Plan. And I am going to go further and say, the way Earth is with the different ills is truly not and was not a part of Earth; Mother Earth's Plan either. And Lovey, if I am wrong about Earth and what I said, truly forgive me and you too Mother Earth because; I am getting into your business.

With that said. Lovey you see to what lengths this race – the White Race will go to lie and deceive including kill here on Earth. No, I shouldn't have to say you see and know because; *THE BIBLE OF MAN IS A TRUE TESTAMENT OF THE LIES THE WHITE RACE TELL ON YOU TO GET HUMANS TO FOLLOW*

THEIR NASTINESS, AND NASTY GOD HERE ON EARTH.

You as God they've made out to be nasty.
A giver backer taker.
An incest loving god.
A thief.
A murderer.
A polygamist loving god.
A god that cannot live by his own rules – laws.
A god that is plain out stupid – inept, and more.

So, you know the lengths these people will go to kill literally here on Earth to their lies and deceit. Thus, their father Satan was the *MASTER OF LIES AND DECEIT. So, as Father is a liar and deceiver, so is his Children and People.*

After that, I had to get up, and I did. Did what I had to do then I was complaining to You Lovey.

Listen everyone.

Yesterday, *did I dream God holding hands?*

Yes, because I changed the original cover of my book, *I NEED ANSWERS GOD.* The first cover was not pleasing to God and I wanted to keep God pissed off because; I refused to change the cover. However, I found the right cover and replaced the one I originally used which was a Lion and a Sheep; Baby Sheep or Lamb.

After complaining to God about White People and locking them out of Earth all around, and more. I dreamt *WHITE AND BLUE BALLOONS COMING DOWN FROM THE SKY AND THIS OLD BROWN/MAHOGANY FURNITURE WITH DRAWS.* I cannot tell you the exact amount of draws, but I believe it was between 4 – 6 draws. The brown/mahogany old furniture was on the ground, and the balloons fell to the ground. I did not pop them open.

I know what this dream means and what God is telling me. *The balloons of white and blue represents the sky and clouds. The old brown/mahogany furniture represent the past; days of old. Evil did come into Earth, and Evil did make Earth its Domain of Destruction and Death.*

Now the question I pose to Lovey again from another book. Why can't we change the environment of Earth so that Evil cannot come into Earth?

Listen People and My True Loved Ones. We know Evil use Blue and White thus, the Blue Sky and White Clouds. So, why can't we change this?

Why can't we not change the Sky from Blue to Yellow or Green?

No not Black because despite their being light in the darkness, I truly do not like darkness day in and day out.

And no, I am not willing to see Brown Clouds. Too blah – dead for me. And sorry Lovey because I know your favourite colour is Brown.

But do we have to have Clouds Lovey?

Can we not make the Sky yellow with no clouds or even transparent?

Our goal is to make everything truly peaceful.
Truly harmonious.
Truly and ever growing up good and true.

A good and true place to live that is void of war and strife; all the ills and negativity of all.

Therefore, there must, and should never ever be without end any type of violence, diseases, war, strife, prejudice, hatred, unjust law and laws, sin, diseases, sickness, ills, negative forces and energy, evil, death. All that is negative that take away from good and true life here on Earth and beyond Lovey we should not have or give access to Earth. Earth need(s) to gain true strength and power so that her outer and inner core repels all forms of negativity and evil.

The sign Mother Earth now put up for all facets of evil, negative energy, negative forces, negative spirits, and negative people should be:

"ALL ACCESS TO EARTH; HER DENIED MORE THAN INFINITELY AND INDEFINITELY MORE THAN FOREVER EVER WITHOUT END CONTINUALLY WITHOUT END."

No Lovey, Mother Earth has and have been through too much at the hands of wicked and evil people here on Earth. It's time all facets of evil be ejected from her come on now.

Did I dream my cousin's daughter?

Yes

Her face was so black that I could not recognize her.

In the dream, I believe she was in England. She was with a friend that wanted to be let in and I would not let them in. I kept the door closed to them, but her friend found another way in therefore, she was able to get in.

My cousin said something to me, and it was upon looking at her closer I realized it was my cousin Cheryl on my mother's side of the family.

We took off our shoes and she was reminding me of the shoes. Trust me, the shoes at the door was not clean including mine – the soul; inside of our shoe. So, I truly do not know what scandal and or, conflict is going to arise in this family to see a rift later on in life and or, very soon. Therefore, I must caution my family to not bring me in their family drama of nastiness. *I do not care for it nor do I give a BLEEP ABOUT DEAD LEF. You want to squabble about DEAD LEF A FI UNNU BUSINESS NOT MINE. LEAVE ME OUT OF IT POINT BLANK AND PERIOD.*

Bleep all of you and your dead lef affairs and business. I do not live for greed nor do I fight fi dead lef. Unbelievable how people fight and carry on over dead lef. Stop come on now.

Family killing family fi dead lef.
Family not speaking to family because of dead lef.
Family arguing with family over dead lef.

WHAT IS NOT GIVEN TO YOU IS TRULY NOT YOURS. WHY THE HELL ARE YOU FIGHTING FOR IT?

BC RED YIE PERIOD.

Therefore, you see the ugliness of people especially some family members for real.

Further, if any in my family want to sever times with me for these books therefore, the dirty soul of our shoes, go right ahead. My family – cousins cutting ties with me means absolutely nothing to me. Your cutting ties with me will never ever faze me, or cause me to cry. All I have to say is, "I AM OF GOD – LIFE THUS, GOD DID FAVOUR ME, AND FOUND FAVOUR IN ME ABOVE ALL OF YOU." Therefore, I am not the one at the Gate and Gates of Hell.

My other dream had to do with a *CARGO SHIP* that carry goods on the sea.

I was on a dock and this Cargo Ship that was overloaded with goods had backed up in the dock. Then it was trying to come out, and its rope which was high up got caught, and the Cargo Ship was moving from side to side. This one yellow van came crashing down beside me and landed in the water.

Still with its rope attached the Cargo Ship continued on its way and you could see goods falling in the sea and or, ocean. Continuing to see what was happening this White man said

I believe to another and or, some one that it's okay, and said something about Germany and or, the German Company that owned them and or, the cargo would handle it I believe and or, could pay and or, would pay for it.

Now this is where everything got different and scary for me.

This Asian Man looked as if he was psychologically sick; deranged with soot on him with a machete came out wielding it. I told him I loved him to calm him down but that did not help. The other gentleman that was with me tried to stop him by telling him to put the machete down but that did not help. He proceeded to self harm himself.

So, I do not know what is going to happen to China and Germany economically, shipment wise when it comes to shipping of goods; cargo via the ocean or sea.

Mental Wise, I do not know with China and their people if something is going to happen to see Men and Woman in China self harming self if not committing Suicide.

There are so many variables that I am so going to leave this dream alone. And I think that is all the dreams I had this morning.

Crazy hey.

It's the afternoon and I did forget some of my dreams I had this morning.

Dreamt I went shopping and when I was ready to check out and put things in my cart I was told by this man and woman that; *"don't you see your cart have not baggage."* When I looked there was no blue and white baggage compartment, and the wheel was broken. So, I could not use my buggy and or, hand cart.

Weird hey. However, I need some things on the road plus; a letter to be mailed, and I cannot go. My back refuse to allow me to go. So, instead; I am sending my son; well paying my last child $10 plus giving him my bus pass to go for me.

Yesterday was not so good for me. I feel down off my chair while putting on my socks. I was not supposed to go on the road, but I ignored my warning signs and decided to go anyway. I had to. I could not put off going to my dad's any longer. Each time I told him I was coming, I would not feel well.

I do need a car to get me from Point A to Point B, but I am not financially stable to get a car therefore, the bus is my only alternative. However yesterday, my son; last child accompanied me to my dad's and got us a ride to go and come for which I was thankful and blessed. My knee was acting up and I think this was due to the fall I had. I am okay thank God. And no, I do not dare tell my doctors I fell. Balance is an issue at times for me.

Oh lord have mercy here I go again with my little tid bits when it comes to me and my happenings.

My other dream that I forgot had to do with *Africa.*

Dreamt I was in Africa. I believe Kenya but I cannot fully tell you the country. This young female was with me and she was feeding me and or, giving me Cut Sugar Cane to eat for which I loved.

Wow because I truly love Sugar Cane.

I can't remember if I asked her if she had Roast Breadfruit. However, she wanted to give me some Chicken – Cured Chicken to eat, and she took me to get the Chicken. Seeing the meat on the ground; some cut in strips; not much, and another big piece. I thought it was pork and she said it's not pork but chicken. She cut a piece of the Cured Chicken for me but discarded the meat; did not give it to me.

So do not know what that dream mean, and I am so going to leave it alone. So hope I get to go to Africa soon, but to the way these *WHITE DEVILS ARE RUNNING THE WORLD, YOU HAVE TO TAKE THEIR VACCINE TO TRAVEL AND I REFUSE TO TAKE THEIR VACCINE. Therefore, their NEW WORLD ORDER THAT THEY ARE IMPLEMENTING SLOWLY BUT SURELY, AND ABSOLUTELY NO ONE IN SOCIETY GLOBALLY IS SEEING THIS – THEIR NEW WORLD ORDER OF LIES, DECEIT, CONTROL, AND ULTIMATE DEATH – THE MASS EXTINCTION OF HUMANS.*

I should not have to comply to the will of the Pharmaceutical Demons of the Globe that design viruses alongside their government to kill. *I have a GOD GIVEN RIGHT AND CONSTITUTIONAL RIGHT TO LIVE FREE AND WITHOUT THE ILLS OF THESE DEMONS HERE ON EARTH. THEREFORE, WHAT WE AS HUMANS ARE FACING DUE TO THEIR COVID-19 LOCK*

DOWN IS NO DIFFERENT FROM SLAVERY AND APARTHEID.

These are the thing humans especially Blacks cannot see. *ABSOLUTELY NO ONE HAS ANY RIGHT OR RIGHTS UNDER WHITE RULE – THEIR APARTHEID REGIME OF GLOBAL CONFLICT; HATE AND DISCRIMATION; MURDER.*

Dear God how I hope *TIME WILL TELL FOR THESE MONSTERS HERE ON EARTH.*

TIME WILL TELL by Robert Nesta Marley, aka Bob Marley.

But then God is powerless here on earth and so is Mother Earth. She too is powerless in her domain because of these people and the atrocities they do in her and get away with it because "SATAN – DID GIVE THEM AUTHORITY TO KILL WHIST LIVING HERE ON EARTH LTERALLY."

I too am powerless like God to evict these Demonic Beings out of Earth; Mother Earth to never ever return in her, or around her, above her, or under her.

Yes, it's days like these I wish I had unlimited power; that *UNLIMITED ENERGY THAT IS OUT THERE AND HOLD LOVEY'S HAND AS WELL AS, MOTHER EARTH'S HAND AND MAKE POSITIVE CHANGES FOR THE BETTER GOOD*

OF EARTH AND THE GOOD AND TRUE OF EARTH. Trust me, all who are wicked, and evil would be gone no questions asked. Yes, I've seen a world; Earth without White People. Truly hope with Life; God will ensure the necessary good changes are made for the good and true where absolutely no one will have to deal with Death – the Children and People of Death of the different families, and races.

My other dream had to do with Paul. I did cut off our friendship indefinitely yet, I am dreaming about him and his son, and this baby that he was putting in a clear bag. I can't remember if yellow was around the baby.

So not going to worry about Paul and his family woes; issues.

My concern is with the ills humans are facing at the hands of the different evil and greedy corporate demons as well as; demonic government leaders that run the world and have, and has imprisoned everyone as well as, *taken our HUMAN RIGHTS, CONSTITUTIONAL RIGHTS, GOD GIVEN RIGHTS, AND MORE FROM US.* Hogs yes, I went there. Hogs that are controlled by demons because they live with demons and have to; *must do the BIDDING AND WILL OF DEMONS.*

Hogs who do not value life. Cannot value life because they have no life here on Earth or in the Spiritual Real with God.

And yes, as God is powerless here on Earth to shut these Demonic Monsters down, I am powerless also.

51

Mother Earth is powerless also. She too have to live with the ills that humans do day in and day out in her, and can't do a damned thing to help herself in evicting these demons out of her literally.

And do not come to me about using the word Hog. *You do not know just how filthy the Pig and or, Hog, or Swine is in the Spiritual Realm.* When someone call you a Hog, it is not nice nor; is it pretty. I know just how filthy the Swine, Pig, or Hog is in the Spiritual Realm therefore, I use the word to denote the nastiness of some that live amongst us here on Earth.

You know, I have to wonder if people can see their sins – the darkness of them that is in them, and is around them?

No, that was a stupid thing to say Michelle. You need not wonder because people truly do not know their Sins thus, they cannot see the darkness around them, and in them. You know what Sins look like thus, many people seem pretty but; they are that ugly.

I so do not want or need this book to get too long. I do not know what to ask God right now. Hopefully later I will have some more things to write.

Editing this book. I am going to ask all in the Black Community Globally this.

"When are we as a Race and People going to start building us positively all around?

"When are we as a Race and People going to stop building other nations and start building us positively all around?"

"When are we as a Race and People going to give back all the dirty god and gods we believe in and accept, and pick up our own Black God, and live good, true, clean, mentally stable, drug free, debt and death free, ever growing up, and more?"

"When are we as a Race and People going to give up our pursuit of other nations and do all that is good and true to pursue our own Black Nations good and true globally?"

"When are we as a Race and People especially us in the West. Lands like, Canada, the United States of America, and lands in Europe like France, Finland, England, Lands in the Caribbean going to take our Wealth, and Health out of these lands, and begin to build Africa including, the Southern Lands of Africa good, true, clean, positive, ever growing good, and more?"

"When are we as a Race and People going to invest right, true, clean, good and wise in us as well as, in Africa?"

"When are we as a Group of People going to come together truthfully, and buy land in Africa, build homes and give homes – these homes to those who are in true need in Africa?"

"When are our doctors, dentists, and nurses going to do good by going to Africa for a week or two and give *their services free of charge thus, serving their people in a good and true way as well as, bringing back truth and goodness to Africa?"*

"When are many Rich Blacks going to stop showing off on their wealth, and do some good for their African Own?"

"When are we as Black People going to have our own Black Internet, Television Studios, Television Stations, Schools, Hospitals, Hotels, and more in Africa thus, getting rid of, and doing away with White Corporate America as well as, build Africa good and true?"

"When are retired Basketball Players going to invest in Africa; have an African Basketball League on the Continent of Africa, and more?"

"We cannot use the word and or, name "African" American, Afro-Canadian, Pan "African", Euro "African" and ignore all of Africa."

"When are we as Black People Globally going to give back White People their religious lies, their lying and deceiving god that is stink; dirty, their nasty and disgusting book – their so-called holy bible and accept – go back to our Clean God that is not based on religion, religious lies, political lies, churches of death, and more, and live good and true, clean, harmonious

and unified with each other so that God can save us, and keep us good and true?"

"When are we as Black People going to appreciate each other?"

Just take a look at the Internet of Man and see just how perverse and disgusting as well as, disgraceful many in the Black Community has become for _"THE GREED OF MONEY AND SELLING THE DEVIL'S AGENDA."_

Thus, many in the Black Community are not Black. They fall under the White Banner of Death. Many hath no soul because they are literally _"BOUGHT AND SOLD."_ Thus, they have no _"AFRICAN OR BLACK WORTH – VALUE."_

Many in the Black Community are so vile then; we have the Gaul as Black People to wonder why God has, and have divorced billions of us literally.

See, _THE NEW BOOK OF KNOWLEDGE BOOK ONE AND TWO_ written by Michelle and Lovey – God.

Michelle

GIVE IT ALL YOU GOT by Beres Hammond

Had to give it all I got. It's 6:46pm and I am home. My son was complaining about having to have to go on the road for me. He said, I should have done this yesterday. I told him everything was not ready in regards to the letter I have to mail. For which the letter involved him as well. I cannot take arguments when it comes to doing things for me so I told him, *"don't bother, I would go myself"* for which I changed my mind about going. My daughter was going to get me a Lift to go and come but like I said; I changed my mind in going. But my mind was telling me to go so eventually I showered and went. I took the bus to go and come. Mind you, my back was not so great, but I managed. I bore the pain and took my little time in walking.

Listen, I am one to be grateful for a ride and yesterday I was grateful for the ride. I refuse to take advantage of people. I got what I needed to get done yesterday and truly thank God and Kaylee.

I bought her lunch, and we went to the dollar store – Dollar Tree, and I paid for whatever she needed there. I have to be me when it comes to reciprocating kindness. I will not forget kindness, nor will I be ungrateful when it comes to kindness. She had a full tank of gas so I could not buy her gas.

My son sometimes gets to me. He could have easily taken the bus and mailed the letter and got me the couple of items I needed. You know what let me forget it because, *I was the one to go do what I needed to do and not him,* and I did do what I needed to do. Therefore, the song above that I gave you.

Oh lord with the amount of complaining I do to God about White People I have to wonder if God get fed up of me at times, or too.

I am so going to rest my back because it is truly enflamed.

Michelle

It's April 16, 2021 and I so cannot remember my dreams. I had this dream about water – clear shallow water. I am not sure if I was in the South Pacific, or Australia but; I think it was somewhere along that region. I was with this young guy. I cannot tell you what he looked like because I did not notice his looks. He took me to this region where the water was shallow, and the water going underground that had a stone inlet above it. This lobster was in the water and it bumped him I believe or was it me. Anyway, the lobster was in the water along with something else that you could not see. It had a green spike, and it pierced the young man that was with me. He did not see when he got pierced. His brother had gotten pierced earlier. And I am so going to leave this dream alone. Somewhere either in Australia or the South Pacific the water is going to be unsafe for swimming. I just have to watch and see.

Wow to clear river water and or, water.

Now Lovey I want and need to end this book. It's still a bit nippy outside, and the Ontario Government has extended their say at home order for another 6 weeks as well as, given the Police authority to stop people on the road and question them as well as, ask them where they live. *TALK ABOUT WHITE PEOPLE EXTENDING THEIR AUTHORITY AND WHITE PRIVILEDGE TO EXERCISE THEIR DEMONIC APARTHEID BELIEFS ON HUMANS.*

If that was Black People doing this. Wow.

The shit White People would say and do. But; when it comes to White People, their evil actions is just to them including others who are conditioned by the White Race.

Yes. *BATTY FALLARAHS.* Thus, *the atrocities and evils White People get away with globally.*

Trust me, F Doug Ford and his authoritarian beliefs. Combat what strain of Covid-19. Why the F don't the lots of you not stop making diseases and weapons that kill?

Why the hell don't the White Race change ALL YOUR UNJUST LAWS OF GLOBAL APARTHEID?

Laws that benefit the wealthy of the White Race. No, the White Race period.

Laws that are unfair and unjust to others, and other nations.

Laws that uphold, and benefit all the wrongs you in the White Race Globally do.

No, don't go off Michelle. Hell is there thus, many truly do not think of their hell in Hell literally once the spirit shed the flesh.

F WHITE PEOPLE PERIOD.

Unnu goh suck…leave it. When did God give any of you the power and authority to lead anyone of Life or anyone here on Earth for that matter?

<u>Your lies and murderous history stand as proof that not one of you are of God but of Death. You're all demons that pry on the living period.</u>

Dyam vampires. Stop creating strife.
Stop building weapons.
Stop making viruses and diseases.
Stop using and abusing Earth.
Stop lying.

Stop using God as a weapon to get away with your evils.

Stop deceiving.

When you begin to do all these, Earth will be better; can come back to so she can expand.

<u>Dyam warmongers that are VOID OF GOD AND TRUE LIFE.</u>

As for the current Prime Minister of Canada his father must be turning in his grave to the way he's running Canada without no authority, and backbone to stand up to the different <u>PHARMACEUTICAL DEMONS AND GOVERNMENT SCIENTIST THAT DEVELOP AND MANUFACTURE VIRUSES, DISEASES, AND WEAPONS TO KILL.</u>

No Lovey I am tired of this RACE OF DEMONS. THEREFORE, I COME BEFORE YOU AND CHALLENGE THEIR AUTHORITY HERE ON EARTH IN GOODNESS AND IN TRUTH WITH YOU, MOTHER EARTH, THE UNIVERSE, AND MORE. Yes, I had to bring the universe into this because of Space, and the lies the White Race tell on Space – the planets.

Now I ask you Lovey and Mother Earth. WHAT PIECE OF LAND OR COUNTRY DID YOU AND MOTHER EARTH GIVE TO THESE WHITE DEMONS HERE ON EARTH TO LIVE?

No, don't test me Lovey because I know you are itching to blast me for that question thus, I will ask you and Mother Earth again.

WHAT PIECE OF LAND OR COUNTRY DID YOU AND MOTHER EARTH GIVE TO THESE WHITE DEMONS HERE ON EARTH TO LIVE?

What power did You Lovey give to the White Race of Demons to rule any race or anything here on Earth?

Yes, my temper is boiling to the fact that; You and Mother Earth let these people get away with all their ills here on Earth, and nothing is truly being done about them. Yet, when we as Black People do. Unnu quick fi punish.

I am pissed because this – all that is happening here in Ontario and Worldwide with the restrictions being imposed JUST TO SELL PHARMACEUTICALS – THEIR STINKING VACCINE THAT HARM PEOPLE, CHIP PEOPLE, GET PEOPLE SICK, KILL PEOPLE, AND MORE IS NOTHING BUT SLAVERY AND APARTHEID.

No Lovey. THIS IS WHITE PEOPLE EXCERCING THEIR EVIL AT WILL AND YOU ARE TELLING ME, YOU WANT TO DEFEND THESE DEMONS WITH MY QUESTION.

HOW DARE YOU STAND UP FOR DEMONS THAT HAVE NO HEART OR MERCY FOR ANY FORM OF LIFE EVERYWHERE.

Now tell me. Are You and Mother Earth going to compensate the people, and the families of the people they've; the White Demons have and has killed in the NAME OF GREED, MONEY, AND DEATH?

Can You and Mother Earth even compensate their lives given their Sin and Good Record?

And don't You dare say, *"HOW DARE YOU?"* Because, You and Mother Earth dare me.

Yes, there is Life and Death. You and Mother Earth know the Children and People of Death cannot be fair or just. Thus, their unjust laws, murderous ways, unclean giving, unclean morals and moral values, their religion, religious beliefs, religious lies, abusive and destructive ways, lies and deceit, and way more negative and sinful things.

Thus, I have to wonder about You Lovey and your Truth when it comes to Good and True Life.

THUS, SLAVERY IS NOT OVER.

APARTHEID WILL NEVER BE OVER AS LONG AS THE MONSTERS OF LIFE – WHITE RACE RULE; HAVE DOMINION OF EARTH.

Neither You or Mother Earth hath the balls and guts to banish these demons out of life, the life of Earth, and from around our good and true people including, waterways.

I have the balls but unfortunately, I have not that unlimited power to do so. *Trust me, if I had that power, HELL AND DEATH WOULD HAVE TO TAKE THEIR WICKED AND EVIL OWN*

NO MATTER THE COLOUR, GENDER, RACE, ETHNICITY, SPIRIT OUT OF EARTH MORE THAN INFINITELY AND INDEFINITELY MORE THAN CONTINUALLY WITHOUT END TO NEVER EVER RETURN.

No Lovey, You and Mother Earth would have no say because; I am exercising my human rights, God given rights to life, and more to not live amongst or with, including, near the wicked and evil of life here on Earth.

YES, I TRULY LOVE SEGREGATION WHERE GOOD SHOULD NOT LIVE AMONGST OR WITH EVIL, OR IN THE LANDS OF EVIL. I refuse to back down from this with You Lovey. I refuse evil beings and people in our Domain. This we must continue to uphold therefore, THIS SEGREGATION MUST HAPPEN HERE ON EARTH.

You and Mother Earth cannot continue to feed the Devil's Own. I refuse this for the both of you because:

EVIL DESTROY AND KILL.
EVIL SPREAD HATE.
EVIL IS HATE.

EVIL IS A DISEASE – CANCER. 6 and 666 thus 24.

EVIL HATH NO VALUE OR MORAL VALUES.
EVIL LIVE TO KILL.
EVIL MUST DESTROY.

EVIL ENACT LAW AND LAWS TO SUIT EVIL.

EVIL CANNOT BE JUST. Nor can their law and laws be just.

EVIL CANNOT BE TRUTHFUL TO LIFE.
EVIL CAN ONLY BE TRUTHFUL TO DEATH.

EVIL CANNOT BE CLEAN. Evil can only be unclean.

Therefore, I refuse the Children and People of Evil and Wickedness in our domain. *Therefore, I COME BEFORE YOU LOVEY AND MOTHER EARTH AND, CHALLENGE THE VALIDITY OF THE WHITE RACE HERE ON EARTH.*

I TRUTHFULLY COME BEFORE YOU LOVEY AND MOTHER EARTH AND, CHALLENGE THE RIGHT OF ALL IN THE WHITE RACE TO LIVE HERE ON EARTH.

I TRUTHFULLY, AND HONESTLY COME BEFORE YOU LOVEY AND MOTHER EARTH AND, CHALLENGE YOU BOTH FOR THE RIGHT AND RIGHTS OF ALL THE GOOD AND TRUE OF EARTH TO LIVE FREE, AND DAMAGE FREE FROM ALL THE ILLS OF THE WHITE RACE.

I TRUTHFULLY, AND HONESTLY COME BEFORE YOU LOVEY AND MOTHER EARTH AND, CHALLENGE ALL THE LAWS OF INJUSTICE SET UP BY THE WHITE RACE, BABYLON; THE DIFFERENT RACES HERE ON EARTH. LAWS THEY FORCE PEOPLE TO FOLLOW.

I TRUTHFULLY, AND HONESTLY COME BEFORE YOU LOVEY AND MOTHER EARTH AND, CHALLENGE THE BOTH OF YOU WHEN IT COMES TO GOOD AND TRUE LIFE FOR THE GOOD AND TRUE HERE ON EARTH.

I TRUTHFULLY, AND HONESTLY COME BEFORE YOU LOVEY AND MOTEHR EARTH AND, CHALLENGE THE BOOK OF MAN – MAN'S HOLY BIBLE, AND THE VALIDITY OF THIS BOOK THAT THEY USE TO GET PEOPLE TO SIN, AND COMMIT ALL MANNER OF EVIL AGAINST LIFE – YOU.

I CHALLENGE THEM THE WHITE RACE.
I CHALLENGE THEM.
I CHALLENGE THEM.

I BOUND THEM ALL TO HELL TO MY ANGER RIGHT NOW AS TO WHAT IS HAPPENING HERE ON EARTH. NO ESCAPE THEY SHOULD HAVE EVER BECAUSE, I SEAL THEM WITH THEIR OWN SEAL OF DEATH. THEIR 666 AND 6666 TO PURE HELL AND CONDEMNATION FOR THE LIES THEY TELL ON LIFE, THE KILLINGS THEY DO HERE ON EARTH, THEIR UNJUST LAWS THEY MAKE INTO LAW AGAINST NOT ONLY THE BLACK RACE BUT TO ALL, AND MORE.

I CHALLENGE THEM, AND THEIR RIGHTS TO LIVE HERE ON EARTH.

I CHALLENGE THEM, AND ANY BOOK THEY SAY THEY HAVE FROM YOU LOVEY BECAUSE; I DISPROVE ANY BOOK THEY SAY THEY HAVE FROM YOU. YOU DO NOT DEAL WITH THE UNCLEAN NOR, WOULD YOU EVER GIVE YOUR POWER TO A BALD HEAD.

This Bob Marley echoed loudly in his song *TIME WILL TELL* when he said; *"Jah would never give the power to a Baldhead."*

I loudly echo this sentiment and words because; "YOU LOVEY SHOWED ME, AND TOLD ME VIA MY DREAM WORLD THAT THE WHITE RACE WAS LOCKED OUT OF YOUR WORLD – KINGDOM." Therefore, I don't have to look any further for the truth HENCE; MINI BOOK, and THE NEW BOOK OF KNOWLEDGE THAT I HAD TO WRITE FOR YOU THUS, YOUR NAME WAS INCLUDED ON THE COVER OF THE BOOK. I DID HONOUR YOU IN THIS WAY BECAUSE, THE TITLE "THE NEW BOOK OF KNOWLEDGE" YOU NEEDED AS A TITLE FOR THE BOOK HENCE YOU GOT IT; 2 BOOKS.

I am fed up man. *Truly fed up of THESE DEMONS THAT THINK THEY HAVE DOMINION OVER ALL LIFE HERE ON EARTH.*

Life is fair and just Lovey come on now. So, why is this RACE CAUSING US AS HUMANS TO LIVE THEIR UNFAIR AND UNJUST WAY, AND YOU AND MOTHER EARTH IS TRULY NOT DOING ANYTHING TO STOP THESE EVIL BEINGS?

THE WHITE RACE IS LOCKED OUT OF YOUR REALM LOVEY, LOCK THEM THE HELL OUT OF EARTH AS WELL. COME TOGETHER TRUTHFULLY, AND HONESTLY WITH MOTHER EARTH AND COMMAND DEATH TO TAKE THEIR WICKED AND EVIL OWN TO HELL – THE PLANET OF DOOM AND GLOOM AS I CALL IT WHERE DEATH, AND THE DEMONS OF HELL RESIDE, AND CAN HAVE THEIR WAY WITH THEM; THEIR WICKED AND EVIL OWN.

I REFUSE YOU AND MOTHER EARTH FROM BEING THE CORNERSTONE, AND HEAD CORNERSTONE FOR THE WICKED AND EVIL.

LET THEM TAKE THEIR RELIGIONS OF EVIL AND DECEIT WITH THEM TOO. I TRUTHFULLY AND HONESTLY STAND BEFORE YOU AND MOTHER EARTH AND, CHALLENGE THE VALIDITY OF ANY RELIGION.

I KNOW FOR A FACT WITHOUT DOUBT YOU DO NOT BELONG TO ANY RELIGIOUS GROUP, NOR ARE YOU AFFILITATED WITH ANY FORM OF RELIGION.

YES, THE LADY OF ZION AND HER CHURCH BUT THIS IS NOT YOU LOVEY. THEREFORE, THE CHURCH OF ZION IS NOT THE SAME AS RELIGIOUS CHURCHES HERE ON EARTH. THERE IS A BIG DIFFERENCE AND WE CANNOT BRANCH, OR PUT THE CHURCH OF ZION, OR ZION WITH ANY RELIGION OR CHURCH PERIOD. IT IS CATEGORICALLY WRONG TO DO SO THUS, I KNOW ZION, AND WHAT ZION STAND FOR.

Everything about the White Race I challenge Lovey in goodness and in truth come on now.

Yes, I am going to go this far and, *CHALLENGE DEATH AS WELL.*

I CHALLENGE DEATH BECAUSE, I WANT AND NEED DEATH TO TAKE THEIR WICKED AND EVIL OWN AND GO.

DEATH HAS AND HAVE AN OBLIGATION TO LIFE AND I AM EXCERCISING MY LIFE RIGHTS WITH DEATH AND TELLING DEATH; ALL FACETS OF DEATH TO TAKE THEIR WICKED AND EVIL OWN AND GO WITHOUT END NEVER TO EVER RETURN TO EARTH EVER AGAIN. AND LOVEY AND MOTHER

EARTH, IF I AM WRONG TO DO THIS; COMMAND DEATH; ALL FACETS OF DEATH TO GO WITH THEIR WICKED AND EVIL OWN TRULY FORGIVE ME BECAUSE LIKE I SAID, I AM FED UP OF THE WHITE RACE OF DEMONS; THAT I HAVE TO LIVE AMONGST HERE ON EARTH DAY IN AND DAY OUT NO MATTER WHERE EVIL RESIDE HERE ON EARTH.

Their laws; the law and laws of the White Race are, and is unconstitutional from a Life and Death standpoint. Therefore, I have no God Given Rights here on Earth with them; the White Race in it because of their Stinking Dominion, and Stinking Bible that people follow to a tee without knowing that the Bible has and have condemned to Hell literally.

The Law of Life and Death specifically states:

"THE WAGES (PAY) OF SIN IS DEATH."

Therefore, Death have to; must take all who are wicked and evil that have more Sin than Good Lovey come on now. Death should not have to wait 24000 years – Earth Years to fully, and truly take their wicked and evil own Lovey come on now.

Come on Lovey. The White Race and Babylon – the Children and People of Babylon have to go to their Domain of Death come on now.

I know Lovey, I should not let my anger get the best of me but, I have to vent to you. I have to come to you with my anger.

I have to tell you everything.
I have to be the true and real me with you come on now.

Come on man Lovey and Mother Earth, *LET TIME TELL FOR THESE DEMONS NUH.*

I HAVE NO TOLERANCE FOR INJUSTICE AND UNFAIRNESS LOVEY COME ON NOW.

Come on Lovey, am I not living in hell because of these people?

Are others not living in hell because of these people and their virus bullshit?

No, Lovey, I need justice.
I am crying out for justice.

No, going down on my knees is a sin when it comes to prayer and talking to You Lovey but; if I have to go down on my hands and knees for you to see me, hear me, initiate true justice for all then so be it. I will do it.

Who the hell are they: the White Race and Babylon to come into Earth and take charge like that?

Who the hell are they to come into Earth and take life from life – You Lovey?

Further, I HONESTLY AND TRUTHFULLY CHALLENGE THEIR JESUS – BLACK DEATH.

Black Death – Jesus is not of life therefore, NO CHILD OF LIFE CAN OR WILL SAVE A CHILD – ANYONE OF DEATH NO MATTER THE RACE, GENDER, COLOUR, OR CREED.

So yes, Lovey; I am tired and still upset.

Tired of lies.
Tired of political lies.
Tired of religious lies.
Tired of medical lies.
Tired of the lies told on space.

Tired of the lies people accept – believe to be the truth of You Lovey.

Tired of the lies people and their religion tell on you Lovey.

Tired of the way humans treat Mother Earth.
Tired of the way humans are destroying Mother Earth.

Tired of the way humans lie to each other.

Tired of the unjust and horrible way and ways humans treat each other.

Tired of some in my family.
Tired of generational lies.
Tired of African Lies, and more.

Now Lovey look at South Africa where Apartheid was implemented, and Blacks could not buy land in certain areas of their own country; the land of their birth and ancestors.

Look at Canada how the Natives are treated poorly. Some do not have adequate housing, clean drinking water, good sanitation, their rights taken from them in their own land.

Look at Jamaica how the buccaneers devastated the land with their whoredom, murder, raping, to the point where Port Royal sank in June of 1692 thus, Port Royal was deemed the wickedest place on Earth thus, making Jamaica MODERN DAY SODOM AND GOMORRAH LITERALLY BECAUSE YOU LOVEY, DID DEEM JAMAICA UNCLEAN LITERALLY.

Look at the United States of America and the evils the Whites has and have done to Blacks, and the different nations of the globe. Yet, Black Americans cannot wake up and get the hell out of Babylon.

Black Americans have been used and abused yet, refuse to leave out of abusive states; lands. So, to me, Black Americans truly love their abuse because; they're like unto dogs. No matter how their Masters' abuse them, THEY ARE STILL

LOYAL TO THEIR MASTERS, THEY STILL BUILD THEIR MASTERS, STILL LIE FOR THEIR MASTERS, STILL LAY WITH THEIR MASTERS, STILL RIDE AND DIE WITH DEATH; THEIR MASTERS.

Look at syphilis the United States Government developed and manufactured in a laboratory and infected Blacks in that country with.

Look at Aids and Ebola they developed in a laboratory and brought to Africa to infect and kill Black Africans then lied and said, "Aids and Ebola" came from Africa.

Look at Crack Cocaine and the devastation it has on the Global Populace of Drug Addicts.

Look at how many Blacks have and has been lynched because of White Lies – lies told on Blacks thus causing innocent Blacks to die.

Look at Namibia and how White Europeans almost wiped out a Nation of People off the face of the planet.

Look at Black Europeans who were eradicated out of life due to the Black Plague.

Look at Global Slavery – the Slavery of Blacks by Whites.

Now tell me, *how many children were raped by the Monsters – Demons of the White Race?*

How many Blacks were murdered at the hands of Monsters – Demons of the White Race?

How many Black Women were raped at the hands of Monsters – Demons of the White Race that wanted Black Women to produce children upon children for the purpose of selling them – children into slavery?

How many fatherless and motherless children were raised by White Witches/bitches?

Now tell me Lovey, *how can you as a God have mercy for the merciless?*

Can you as God and Good God justify the actions of the White Race?

Can anyone justify the actions of the White Race apart from them?

So now tell me. How fair and just is this nation – the Nation of Whites to anyone here on Earth?

Yes, some will hate me for my words because to them their actions are right and just. But right and just to who?

Has any White stopped to see their injustice?

Isn't their injustice and unfair treatment of others their right and justice to them?

How many will hold up the Bible and use their Demonic Book to justify their actions?

Now tell me Lovey. <u>ARE LIARS AND THIEVES CAPABLE OF THE TRUTH?</u>

Aren't their lies and deceit not the truth to and for them?

No truly don't because I am so not finished with You yet.

Now, <u>LOOK AT YOU LOVEY.</u>

Now tell me, <u>ARE YOU PLEASED WITH THE LIES THE WHITE RACE TELL ON YOU IN THE NAME OF RELIGION, AND IN THEIR SO-CALLED HOLY BOOK; THEIR BIBLE, AND DIFFERENT BIBLES?</u>

<u>WERE YOU AS OUR BLACK GOD, SUSTAINER, CREATOR, CARE GIVER, MAINTAINER, AND MORE NOT TAKEN FROM US?</u>

<u>WERE YOU NOT DRIVEN OUT OF EARTH?</u>

<u>WERE WE AS BLACK PEOPLE NOT GIVEN ANOTHER GOD?</u>

<u>A GOD THAT IS AS NASTY AS WHITE PEOPLE.</u>

A GOD THAT IS AS VALUELESS AS WHITE PEOPLE.

A GOD THAT IS AS SPITEFUL AS WHITE PEOPLE.

A GOD THAT HATE BLACK PEOPLE AS WHITE PEOPLE HATE BLACK PEOPLE.

A GOOD THAT IS JEALOUS OF BLACK PEOPLE THEREFORE, THEIR GOD, THEIR SO-CALLED HOLY BIBLE, AND THE DEMONS THAT COMMAND THEM TO KILL; TELL THEM WHAT TO DO, AND MORE. THUS, THEIR KILLING SPREES HERE ON EARTH AND, THE DIFFERENT ARMIES OF DEATH GLOBALLY HERE ON EARTH.

A GOD THAT IS SO FILTHY THAT BLACK PEOPLE HAVE AND HAS BOWED DOWN TO THEM – THE NASTY GOD THE WHITE RACE GAVE US; THEM.

No, truly don't go there because I too want to cry but I refuse to cry in this way for you, and for our Children and People because many refuses to break away from the White Man's way of lies and nastiness - Hell.

Now tell me Lovey, how many will call me racist.

How many will say I hate White People?

How many will stand by their White Oppressors, and lift them up because of these words?

How many Blacks will justify White Lies?

How many Blacks will justify the White Man's Book – so-called Holy Bible?

Do Blacks even know that when we accept the "<u>WHITE MAN'S WAY OF LIFE, WE FORFEIT ALL LIFE WITH YOU LOVEY?</u>

This is why we as Blacks go around in Circles of Confusion thinking Religion will save us when in fact; Religion takes you further away from us Lovey.

When we as Black People go down on our knees to pray, we are praying to Death and not You Lovey.

As Black People, we do not know that; when we as Black People go down on our knees to pray God do walk away from us. <u>God do take his life from us by divorcing us from life – his life.</u>

Now tell me Lovey. "When are we as Black People going to have our own <u>BLACK; FULLY BLACK OWNED AIR LINES, AIR STRIPS, AND AIRPORTS</u> that we travel on thus, building us globally?

Thus, Blacks truly do not know that when we support our enemies; those who are not of you Lovey, "we take away our blessings and prosperity from us." Thus, giving our enemies ownership and glory over us – our life and wealth.

Now go back to our roots Lovey and tell me:

OVER THE YEARS AND CENTURIES; HOW MANY BLACKS GLOBALLY HAVE AND HAS DEFENDED YOU, OR EVEN KNOW ABOUT YOU?

No, I am keeping it full hundred with you Lovey.

It's not what's good for the goose is good for the gander. All are cooked and eaten period.

This is life Lovey. Our life as a Race and People.

Look at you Lovey and tell me, *WAS THE BIBLE OF MAN WARRANTED?*

YOU AS GOD THE WHITE RACE LIED ON. WHAT SAY WE/US HERE ON EARTH?

Now look at Earth, You Mother Earth because you are included in this as well.

Now tell me, *ARE NUCLEAR WEAPONS NECESSARY?*

WAS THE A BOMB NECESSARY?

WAS THE DIFFERENT WARS OF MAN – MEN WARRANTED?

ARE THE CHEMICALS THAT ARE DUMPED IN THE WATERWAYS GLOBALLY NECESSARY?

ARE THE DISEASED AND VIRUSES THAT MAN MAKE NECESSARY?

ARE THE CHEMICALS THAT WE SATURATE OUR FOOD SOURCE AND SUPPLY WITH NECESSARY?

Look at how many of the waterways are contaminated in you Mother Earth. Now tell me, *are you pleased with the way in which HUMANS HAVE AND HAS MADE YOU UNCLEAN – DIRTY IN THE NAME OF GREED AND THEIR NASTINESS – DIRTINESS?*

Now tell me Mother Earth. Is it fair to you that all you have given to sustain and maintain humans in you, humans has and have used against you?

Are doing all to destroy and kill you.

Are ungrateful when it comes to you and your goodness.

Are truly unclean because they cannot keep you clean or truly clean.

Now tell me, *WAS DEATH WARRANTED IN YOU?*

Why do you have to house the Flesh and Spirit of Death including Death's Wicked and Evil Own?

Now tell me, *with the destructive ways of humans and the way they are destroying you, are you pleased?*

Now Lovey let me bring the Universe into this because, you and I both know that the Universe – Outer Space is truly not pleased with the White Race and the LIES THE WHITE RACE TELL ON THE UNIVERSE – OUTER SPACE.

You and I Lovey know that the Universe – Outer Space want this race of people because if it's one thing you do not do is, *tell lies on Space – Outer Space; the Universe, and You Lovey.*

Lovey I do not know what destruction or plan, the Universe and or, Out Space have for the White Race, but I know it is something that is not pretty.

No, I truly do not want or need to be White because, Outer Space patiently awaits them to enact revenge for the lies they tell on Outer Space.

You Lovey from my perspective condone the *LIES THE WHITE RACE TELL ON YOU FROM A PHYSICAL AND SPIRITUAL PERSPECTIVE*.

Mother Earth is truly no different. *It seems as if she too condones THE LIES AND DESTRUCTIVE NATURE OF THE WHITE RACE.*

Therefore, Earth has and have become the Valley of Death, and the Dead Physically come on now.

Now tell me Lovey. Without freedom how can we live?

If our rights and freedom is/are being taken from us, how can we live or be free?

The lies went as far as you Lovey and still this demonic race – all who condone the evils of this race is truly not falling; why?

Now I ask you Lovey. What is so special about the White Race that You and Mother Earth let them get away with all their evils?

And please do not tell me *"TIME."*

Now I ask. Does Death have you by the balls Lovey because, I know Death has and have Earth by her Vagina and yes balls because, *she has not the power to evict all facets of evil from her.*

Evil is destructive thus the force and pull of evil I know.

Oh God Lovey, *why can't TIME TELL FOR WHITE PEOPLE; ALL WHO ARE WICKED AND EVIL HERE ON EARTH?*

No Mother Earth, *LOOK AT HOW UGLY YOU'VE BECOME DUE TO HUMANS.*

Yu nuh pretty nuh more. Yu ugly lacka sin because humans made you that defiled and ugly, and you've done absolutely nothing truthfully and constructively to clean yourself up from the destruction, and destructive ways of humans in you.

And I am going to stop here for now.

Michelle

It's a new day Lovey and I am still angry. You are not replying to me and this is not good. Mother Earth responded. It's as if she is going to burn. No, not her, but it's as if the earth; lands in her globally is going to burn. Earth; the land of Earth; her is going to be like a volcano. So, I do not know if more volcanos are going to erupt because I did not see fire, rain, or anything of that nature.

The land was white and patchy I believe from the dream.

I will not worry about this Lovey. Mother Earth need good and positive change in her and for herself and, however she makes these changes for her is truly up to her. She has feelings and humans truly do not respect her to the mess they have and has caused in her.

Why should humans leave her; Mother Earth dirty?

Why should humans continue to abuse her; Mother Earth?

Now tell me Lovey. *What dirtiness does Mother Earth give humans?*

Is it not humans that give all that is dirty – unclean to Mother Earth and You Lovey?

Come on Lovey I know the value of a Mother therefore, what humans are doing to her; Mother Earth is wrong.

No Lovey, this is *PARENT ABUSE.* Look at the goodness Earth; Mother Earth has and have given us as humans and in return; we abuse and take advantage and disadvantage of her; Mother Earth; why?

I am building you good and true, I am kind to you, I uplift you, I give you all you want and need in life, build me good and true tu nuh come on now?

Why destroy me and I am good to you?

Keep the goodness going so that we can grow good and true together.

Cherish me like I cherish you come on now.

EARTH; MOTHER EARTH BUILDS BUT, HUMANS TUMBLE DOWN – DESTROY. There are no ands ifs or buts about this Lovey and Mother Earth come on now.

Now I am dreaming him again. Him complaining to the Woman of Zion. I was with my last child and he – him, the wicked and evil dead was complaining to the Woman of Zion because; in real life she knew him too. Shi a biyah im. Now let me tell you this Lovey because I woke up out of my dream and swore. Im BC wutless.

Was worthless in life, and still worthless because he's worthless in death.

No Lovey because, *if the Woman of Zion OPEN HER DOOR TO EVIL AND LISTEN TO THEM. SHUT HER THE HELL DOWN AND EVICT HER ASS FROM LIFE AS WELL AS ZION WITHOUT HESITATION.*

Listen to me and listen to me well and good Lovey. *I will not have her or anyone of life listening to evil petition them for mercy, forgiveness, sympathy, anything to do with life or them. I know how abusive evil is.*

I know how destructive evil is. Just look at Earth.

Look at all the evil Evil has and have caused here on Earth.

Look at the way Evil has gotten billions here on Earth to forfeit life with you Lovey.

I know how evil lie because evil is the master of lies and deceit thus, Satan and his Children and People no matter the race or gender.

Evil destroy all who are good. You, me, Mother Earth, and more are a testament to the levels evil will go to gain sympathy, access to life, and once evil has and have gained access to your life and world, *evil do all to destroy and kill you* therefore, if the Woman of Zion think she is going to get away with his bullshit of lies, she had better think again. Shut Zion the hell down then Lovey come on now.

Remember the Young Black Girl and what she said to her friend about getting access to his Pin Number and how she would clean out his Bank Account.

Lovey, this is how heartless, valueless, and worthless some in the Black Community Globally has and have become.

Now:
What about his bills?
Rent
Food

Lovey, how can you look at nastiness such as these?

Therefore, not all that hath Black Hue are Black – fall under the Black Banner of Life literally. Valueless and worthless; without moral and moral values are some literally.

So, in all I do Lovey. I will not, and cannot have evil returning anywhere in life where good and true life is come on now. Let this be the end of all who are wicked and evil come on now.

I don't need anymore pain.

Mother Earth do not need anymore pain.
You Lovey do not need anymore pain.

The good and true of Earth do not need anymore pain.

Let it all be done for evil because You, Me, and Mother Earth see just how destructive and deadly evil is. Evil did turn the soil, waters, the land; earth; dirt of Earth against humans, and Mother Earth herself.

Look at the Nuclear Testing that is done here on Earth that has and have caused certain areas to be contaminated. So contaminated that lands is/are inhabitable.

Man did contaminate the waterways of life.

Man did contaminate the soil of earth using chemicals in their crops – ground provisions, and more.

Humans did become destroyers, and are the destroyers of Life, and this Earth Lovey come on now. Yet, we want life. Therefore, the Continental Rift and or, Shift must take place. Humans cannot continue on their path of destruction come on now.

Now look at it Lovey and be truthful to self.

Look at how hard I've prayed and cussed you out for things in life.

Look at how hard I have to struggle.
Look at how hard I have it Financially.
Look at how hard I have it Death Wise.
Look at how hard I have it Health Wise.
Look at how hard I have You Lovey Wise.
Look at how hard I have it Travel Wise.
Look at how hard I have it Earth Wise.

I need to plant good and true and cannot plant because, there are obstacles in my way; why?

You're not moving these obstacles out my way because, it's as if you don't know me in my view yet, you asked me to write you a book. I did though it took some time. I did that which was required of me yet, You Lovey cannot do that which you required of me here on Earth; why?

Why do you dilly dally when it comes to RIGHTEOUSNESS?

Why do you not listen to me?

Why ask me to do something then not make the necessary changes that is required right away?

The good and true here on Earth should not starve for you Lovey come on now.

The good and true here on Earth should not have to wait in vain for you Lovey come on now.

The good and true should not have to be subject to the ills and ill happenings of others; those who belong to Death here on Earth come on now.

The good and true should, and need to have *TRUTH AND JUSTICE* here on Earth for us.

The good and true should always have You Lovey and Mother Earth as our good and true keep, and source continually without end come on now.

The good and true of life should not have varying law and laws. We should, and have fair and true law and laws that govern us truthfully. We cannot have, and should never ever have this set of laws and that set of laws for this race and that race because in our land and lands with You and Mother Earth Lovey, we are one people living under the same roof – Your Roof and Mother Earth's Roof therefore, we have to respect the law and laws set up for us. Laws that are truly just and fair.

No Lovey, there are no unjust anything in our land and lands, and you know this. We have to be right and exact; fair and just all the time come on now. You know how I feel about Life and Truth; You, and Mother Earth, and the Waterways of Life yet, you continually ignore me.

It's time for you to get off your ass and do that which is right and true; just for our good and true of Earth. Mother

Earth is changing – going to change drastically therefore, we need to secure our good and true of life Land Wise, Food Wise, Water Wise, Health Wise, You Wise, Mother Earth Wise, Family Wise, and More.

We have to and must abandon the White Way of Life and Living because this way; the White Way of Life, and Living is truly not Life come on now.

We need to; have to live good and true here on Earth Lovey come on now.

<u>NO MORE TIME ALLOTTED TO DEATH HERE ON EARTH COME ON NOW MAN.</u>

I am tired and I truly do not know why **_BEAUTIFUL_ by Romain Virgo** is in my head. Now I am listening to this song.

Now Lovey and Mother Earth. Are the both of you not tired of the happenings here on Earth?

I need true beauty and truth in my life, and I cannot have this here on Earth living amongst the Wicked and Evil including some of my children. Therefore, evil need to be shut down and left powerless here on Earth. We cannot continue to allow the heartless to destroy it all.

Thus yes, <u>_I WILL CONTINUE TO CHALLENGE THE WHITE RACE BECAUSE THEY ARE NOT A VALID RACE IN MY VIEW. Meaning, THEY DID NOT CREATE EARTH OR THE UNIVERSE THEREFORE, THEY SHOULD NOT BE ALLOWED TO DESTROY IT._</u>

No Lovey, *NO WHITE PERSON CAN VALIDATE LIFE.*

NOT EVEN THEIR HUE – SKIN COLOUR CAN VALIDATE LIFE, AND I AM NOT BEING RACIST THOUGH I SEEM RACIST.

Yes, I know I should not have said that because the Blackman's hue cannot validate life beyond the Realm of Life or in Life. You do not base life on the colour of skin; anyone's hue.

And I am so going to leave well enough alone because, I know I am overstepping my boundaries with you Lovey when it comes to speaking about hue. But You Lovey as God have to, and must do that which is true, truly true, right, truly right, just, truly just, good, truly good, positive, truly positive, ever growing good, truly good and true for the good and true of Earth only as well as, for Mother Earth.

Death got what they needed. Now let it be over. Do not continue on with the choice of Man; Humans because you can clearly see that *BILLIONS DO NOT ADHERE TO GOOD AND TRUE LIFE.*

Many could care less about life because in truth, billions truly do not know the Truth of You and Life Lovey including, the truth of Mother Earth.

LIFE CANNOT GAIN LIVING IN DECAY LOVEY COME ON NOW.

LIFE CANNOT GROW LIVING IN AND AMONGST SIN; THE WICKED AND SINFUL AND YOU KNOW THIS FOR A FACT WITHOUT DOUBT LOVEY COME ON NOW.

LIFE ISN'T ABOUT DEATH. LIFE IS ABOUT GOODNESS AND TRUTH, AND LIVING LIFE GOOD AND TRUE COME ON NOW.

Lovey, *"the life we live here on Earth determines where we go once the spirit shed the flesh."* Humans did make the choice to do evil. The White Race has and have proven this to you that they've chosen Evil over Good. So, let their empire crumble here on Earth. The White Race hath no place with You in the Spiritual Realm Lovey therefore, let them have no place here on Earth either with You and Mother Earth. Right is right, and fair is fair come on now.

Listen Lovey, *"you never gave anyone here on Earth a toxic life to live by."*

Mother Earth "did not give anyone human or anything for that matter, a toxic life or lifestyle to live by."

We as humans are the ones to make life; "the life of all toxic here on Earth" come on now. Therefore, humans cannot live right or true.

Babylon is not of life.

The White Race is not of life.

Many in the Black Race is truly not of life.
Many in the Chinese Race is truly not of life.

So let these people go and separate as well as, *segregate the Good from the Bad; Wicked and Evil.*

INTEGRATION DO(ES) NOT WORK.

Integrating with evil is a sin. An abomination unto Life and you know this Lovey yet, you refuse to separate and segregate our good and true people from those of the wicked and evil. Why?

When you integrate with evil you take on the sin and sins of evil.

When you integrate with evil you become evil because you have to do the will of evil.

Evil do beat you into submission. *This I know for a fact without doubt.*

Evil dominate.
Evil abuse you.
Evil destroy you.
Evil Control.
Evil write laws to suit evil.
Evil do kill.

You cannot say, You *"Love So"* Lovey and keep your people; our people here on Earth integrated with evil; the wicked and evil of Earth. It just do(es) not work, nor is it just or right.

Why *"LOVE US SO,"* and let us take on the Sins of Evil; the Wicked and Evil of this Earth?

No, don't be shocked. You Lovey should be looking at things in this way. You cannot continue to let us take on the Sin and Sins of the Wicked and Evil. This is truly not fair nor is it just for our good and true including, me to have to take on the Crimes; Sins of Others.

You cannot *"LOVE US SO,"* and not protect us from the ills, and ill will of the wicked and evil.

You cannot *"LOVE US SO,"* and leave us; our good and true to live, and die with the heartless.

You cannot *"LOVE US SO,"* and not prepare a good and true place for us; the good and true here on Earth to live without the constraints of the wicked and evil.

You cannot *"LOVE US SO,"* and not set up impenetrable frames and frameworks including, impenetrable foundations with us the good and true so that evil; no form of evil, negative energy, negative spirits can impact our life, and take us away from you ever again Lovey come on now. Now let me ask you something Lovey.

"Do you have a Court of Law that I can lodge all my complaints in apart from You because; You are truly not listening to me?"

95

I need the Court of Life Lovey because, I have many issues that need resolving, and You are truly not resolving them. Therefore, I have to go above you if that's possible to go above you.

You cannot *"LOVE US SO,"* and not set up true guidelines for Earth; You and Mother Earth to follow; adhere to all the time when it comes to *GOOD AND EVIL* come on now. And, do not say guidelines are set up here on Earth thus, Life, and Death. Thus, *"THE LIFE YOU LIVE HERE ON EARTH DETERMINE WHERE YOU GO ONCE THE SPIRIT SHED THE FLESH."*

Those are my words and truth Lovey. Thus, you are truly correct. But Lovey, did You and Mother Earth have to make Earth; all of Earth become so lawless; the Valley of Death?

Did You and Mother Earth have to make Good be integrated with all Evil?

Yes, Life is physical and spiritual and so is Death. But in Death being physical and spiritual, not all has and have chosen Death for self here on Earth.

Now tell me this Lovey. Did you hand over Earth to Death and this is why and or, one of the reasons you are gone from Earth?

I made my choice of goodness and truth. It is now for you Lovey to adhere to this goodness and truth not just in your realm; world, *but on Earth also.*

No one can have life living in debt and death Lovey come on now.

Looking at you from a different perspective and given what is happening here on Earth. Your *"LOVE US SO"* is truly not Life. It is Death.

Your *"LOVE SO"* is truly not helping me in the areas I strongly need help in.

You cannot say, you *"LOVE US SO,"* and not be there for our good and true people.

You cannot say, you *"LOVE US SO,"* and shut the door in our face; the face and faces of the good and true come on now.

You cannot say, you *"LOVE US SO,"* and not prepare a good and true place for us to live here on Earth come on now. A place that is truly peaceful, truly harmonious, truly beautiful with crystal clear waters that cannot be tainted and polluted; land space that we can plant organically, and all out grow up to You *GOOD AND TRUE, HONEST, CLEAN, PURE, and more good and true things that are positive in life all around.*

Oh man, I so don't want this book to end. I want and need to continue writing therefore, please permit me Lovey to have a Part Three to this book.

Yes, I want to tackle the Jamaican Government, but I am going to leave Jamaica to the Hog that governs them, and has and have sold them out fi piece of bulla alone.

No Lovey. Have you seen the State of Jamaica?

No, I should not ask you that because, <u>You did deem Jamaica unclean,</u> an ole people sey; "<u>wha gaane bad a mauning caane cum good a evening."</u> Therefore, Jamaica and the People of Jamaica is fully gone. Has and have turned from life thus, <u>DEMONS RUN THE LAND LITERALLY. No amount of good anyone does on the land can bring back Jamaica from Death – the DEBT THAT IS OWED TO FEMALE BLACK DEATH.</u>

So no, let me stay away from the Politics – no, <u>POLITRICKS; THE TRICKS OF MAN – MEN.</u>

Michelle

Yes Lovey, people will think me racist and that I hate White People like I said earlier on to what I wrote. This is fine for people to think this way. It is their right and belief. However, I cannot hate White People. I am not them. Thus, *many cannot see their wrongs.*

Many cannot walk in the shoes of Blacks.

Many truly do not care how Blacks are treated, or the way they treat You and Mother Earth Lovey.

Now let me ask you Lovey. For their murderous ways here on Earth. Can anyone in the White Race pay for the debts of the White Race with any good they've done?

Can anyone in the White Race compensate anyone for the lives they've taken here on Earth Lovey?

Can anyone in the White Race or any Race compensate you Lovey for the lives they've taken from You in the name of greed, lies, hate, religion, politics, and more and given to Death?

Who here on Earth can compensate You Lovey for Life?

What many truly do not realize, or want to know is that; *LIES ARE SINS.*

The White Race is locked out of Life therefore, they had to lie; do all for humans to FORFEIT LIFE WITH GOD – LIFE.

The Lies of the White Race is/are the Lies of the White Race. Therefore, I do not know why Blacks have to be Jesus all around for White People, and forfeit their life with you Lovey for Death.

Why give up Life for Death?

Why not live good and true so that when the Spirit shed the Flesh you go up to see God with your Good Record?

Black People. When you forfeit your life here on Earth to Death, that's it for you. You cannot be saved. Therefore know:

"THERE IS NO JESUS BANK WITH GOD." If you have no Savings with God, God cannot save you. There are no ands, ifs, or buts about this.

The White Race did forfeit Life thus, causing their White Own to forfeit life with God also. Therefore, many do not know that when they go to church – any church to praise God, they are praising Death, and bowing down to Death.

Full truth is Lovey. I truly do not need dominion over them; anyone or Earth.

I do not need strife with them; anyone here on Earth, or anywhere for that matter.

I do not need hate in my life. I need life all around to be just, fair, unbiases, not one sided, or unbalanced, and more.

Right now, the Justice System of Man Globally is truly not fair, nor is it balanced. You cannot have one set of rules; laws for this race, and that race. Nor can you hate a Nation of People based on Skin Colour come on now.

Demonic Laws – the Law and Laws of Men should not take precedence over Truth; Right and True Justice period. This is why I tell you Lovey *to LET DEATH GO WITH THEIR WICKED AND EVIL OWN.* It is not fair nor is it just for Death's Children and People to be integrated with the Good and True of Life. You are taking Life from the Good and True when you continue to let us; the Good and True be integrated with the Wicked and Evil; Death's True Own, and Own.

LIFE CANNOT HAVE BALANCE AS LONG AS THERE IS INJUSTICE AROUND LOVEY COME ON NOW.

EARTH CANNOT HAVE BALANCE AS LONG AS UNJUST PEOPLE; HUMANS CONTINUALLY RAPE HER OF HER SELF WORTH, WORTH, AND INTEGRITY COME ON NOW.

Now I was talking to you while I was doing dishes, and you were not pleased with me when I compared you to Krishna, Buddha, the different gods that is out there. Thus, I know without doubt that it is categorically wrong; a sin for anyone to compare you to the different gods of Man – the different races.

Now Lovey. When I think of the Black Race over time from then until now. Is it not the Black Race that is the Eliminated Race?

Is it not Blacks that has and have been suffering?
Is it not Blacks that are the hated here on Earth?

Now tell me Lovey. <u>WHICH RACE HAS AND HAVE SUFFERED MORE HERE ON EARTH OTHER THAN THE BLACK RACE AND YES, YOU, AND MOTHER EARTH?</u>

Babylon did take Blacks from you.
Whites – Satan's own did take Blacks from you.

And to be fair and just. Some Blacks did take self; themself from you Lovey.

<u>Now tell me Lovey. How much more of our people are the different races including, our evil Black Own going to take – kill?</u>

What will it take for Black People to wake up and stop dividing themselves?

What will it take for Black People to wake up and stop dividing themself into tribes thus, their Tribal Wars that has and have killed many of their Black Own?

Lovey, let me now ask you this.

When will the White Race open their eyes and know for a fact without doubt that <u>"THE WHITE</u>

RACE BASED ON HUE AND EVIL DEEDS IS LITERALLY HELL BOUND?"

When will they finally see and know that there is truly no escaping "HELL" for them?

What will it take for Black People to wake up and stop killing self, and each other?

What will it take Lovey to bring our good and true people home to you safely?

We can no longer stay divided and be divided as a Race and People Lovey come on now.

Right now, you are truly not listening to us. And I am going to go there with this song and truly forgive me because you are truly not Jesus – Black Death who was crucified.

Yes, I know Jesus did not exist because; YOU AS GOOD GOD AND ALLELUJAH WOULD NEVER EVER MAKE SACRIFICES UNTO DEATH. NOR, WOULD YOU ALLOW ANY CHILD OF LIFE TO SACRIFICE THEMSELF UNTO DEATH TO SAVE DEATH'S WICKED AND EVIL OWN.

But I going to go there with TAKE ME TO THE KING *by Tamela Mann.*

Listen to her truth when she said; "truth is."

Now Lovey, IF WE CANNOT COME TO YOU FOR EVERYTHING; WHERE WILL, AND MUST WE TURN?

WHAT ARE YOU LEAVING US TO DO HERE ON EARTH?

YOU AS OUR BLACK GOD WAS TAKEN FROM US.

WE WERE LEFT BROKEN
UNATTENED TO
SHATTERED
RAPED AND ABUSED
LEFT TO DIE

Now look at what we have to go through to find you.

We have become desperate and hopeless because, **the GOD WE ARE GIVEN TO SERVE HERE ON EARTH IS TRULY NOT YOU.**

Coming to you is our option but, **NOT ONE OF US CAN COME TO YOU CLEAN BECAUSE OF WHAT WE ACCEPT, AND BELIEVE IN HERE ON EARTH COME ON NOW.**

So, tell me, **WHAT IS LEFT OF US APART FROM DEATH.**

HAVE YOU NOT LEFT US TO DIE AT THE HANDS OF DEATH COME ON NOW?

HOW CAN WE HAVE HOPE WHEN OUR TRUE AND GOOD HOPE HAS AND HAVE LEFT US TO DIE LIKE DOGS?

No Lovey, be true and fair.

Have you not turned you BACK ON THE BLACK RACE?

How many of us have you answered truthfully here on Earth?

And truly don't look at me because I am still quarreling with you, and asking you questions for which you have categorically ignored. Therefore, you have left me lost and confused here on Earth in so many ways.

When you leave us Lovey, what do you expect from us?

Will we not turn to all that is ill – wicked and evil?
Will we not continue to dirty ourself?

Will we not think you have abandoned us?
Will we not continue to sin reckless and rude?

How much more shall, and should we run around in circles like a dog trying to get at its tail?

How much more should we feel abandoned, used, abused, shackled and chained, worthless, valueless, and more when it come to You Lovey?

No Lovey, **WHAT MORE SHALL WE DO?**

We cannot go down on our knees and come to you.

I cannot plea with you anymore.

I truly cannot because you are truly not hearing me. Nor are you adhering to the words in these books.

Yes, I am hurt but Earth can no longer be the Valley of Death. Many of us – me especially want and need an escape from the evils of this Earth come on now.

HOW MUCH MORE SHOULD I WRITE AND CONFESS TO YOU?

HOW MUCH MORE TRUTH CAN I GIVE YOU FOR YOU TO SEE AND HEAR ME?

HOW MUCH MORE OF ME SHOULD I GIVE OF ME FOR YOU TO HEAR AND SEE ME?

HOW MUCH MORE SONGS MUST I OFFER AND GIVE YOU FOR YOU TO HEAR ME?

Now tell me Lovey. **WHO IS THE ONE TO BE PLAYING GAMES WITH PEOPLE'S LIVES HERE ON EARTH?**

It's not Death. It is You Lovey.

You are the one to be playing games and ripping the lives of the Good and True apart here on Earth. Therefore, life with you is lopsided come on now.

YOU CANNOT SEE OUR PAIN AND HOPELESSNESS LOVEY COME ON NOW AND DO NOTHING TO HELP US INCLUDING, ME. And in all honesty, I think you refuse to see our pain and hurt here on Earth. You do not have to be privy to the pain and hurt we are feeling because, <u>YOU LOVEY ENSURED YOU SEPARATED YOURSELF FROM THE LIFE OF EARTH PERIOD.</u>

If you are not healing us, how can we continue to look to you for good and true salvation; saving?

My son interrupted me and now I have lost my train of thought. I wanted to say something of importance to you Lovey but now I cannot ask because, I forgot what I wanted to say.

But Lovey, we are weary.

Now let me ask you this and to fair and just to you Lovey. <u>APART FROM US AS BLACKS – MANY BLACKS ABANDONING YOU LOVEY FOR DEATH, WHAT OTHER ATROCITY DID WE AS BLACKS DO FOR YOU TO LEAVE US TO DEATH FOR DEATH TO HAVE THEIR WAY WITH US AS A RACE AND PEOPLE FROM THEN UNTIL NOW INCLUDING, TOMORROW?</u>

I know Death is truly not better than life hence Blacks have has and truly felt it and still, <u>WE STILL CANNOT LEARN FROM OUR ILLS, THE MISTAKES WE MAKE, THE HATRED TOWARDS US AS A RACE AND PEOPLE, THE WAY WE ARE USED AS GUINEA PIGS AND SCAPEGOATS, AND MORE FOR THE DIFFERENT RACES GLOBALLY.</u>

Yes Lovey, I know we can no longer continue to forfeit life with you. As Blacks, we fail to see that all is happening to us globally is truly do to us.

When we as Black People forfeit life with God – Lovey, Lovey – God leave us to the abuse we accept. So, however Death and the Children and People of Death use and abuse us, is truly up to Death and the Children and People of Death. Slavery, all that is unjust, unbalanced, unclean, evil, dirty, is what we get when we give up our Black God for the nastiness of other gods. So, now you as Blacks know some of the truth. Well, the knowledge and truth I know.

Further know. It only takes one to allow evil into your land.

Once the dirty and unclean gain access to your land – country; you as people of your land – country has and have dirtied you and your land as well as, taken on the Sin and Sins of that dirty and unclean person. Thus, Death has and have entered your land. Therefore, it is imperative you know who you give access to your land and lands.

Michelle

Now Lovey. If the Tamela Mann's song TAKE ME TO THE KING did not get to you in some way then; look at the Jamaica Animated Comedy Video by Las May Toon.

The video is:
YARDIE RUNNINGS #44 HELP FROM HEAVEN.

Look how the old man prayed and prayed and asked you for help.

Just watch the video Lovey.

Now, at the end of the video isn't that truly you even though he thought the people in the Post Office cheated him.

All in all Lovey, you did have mercy on him and helped him.

Now Lovey. Do I not complain to you so much?

Man I truly love this video because this is me with you at times.

Lovey talking to you do not work.

Look at how many books I've written under the Michelle Jean banner of books, and it seems I am still quarrelling with you for Justice. You are not reading these books nor are you hearing me; why?

Wow because as God you truly know how to shut people out for real.

But despite it all Lovey, truly thank you because; you are truly there in some way for me.

Therefore, your word have to be sincere and true when you are blessing us.

Yes, I know your blessing is water thus, Earth has and have an abundance of Water.

Wow.

Michelle

It's April 18, 2021 and I am listening to *BE OF GOOD COURAGE by Luciano the Reggae Artist.*

Today, I have to be of good courage because; I don't think I read it right that; in order for the *PEOPLE OF ST. VINCENT TO TRAVEL THEY HAVE TO BE VACCINATED.*

No. Don't swear Michelle because *A NATION OF PEOPLE ARE BEING HELD HOSTAGE BY THE DEMONIC PHAMACEUTICAL COMPANIES, AND THE DIFFERENT INEPT AND CORRUPT POLITICIANS OF THE DIFFERENT LAND THAT PUT MONEY AND GREED OVER THE NEEDS – URGENT NEED AND NEEDS OF OTHERS.*

No Lovey.

Man, I wish Mother Earth would completely stop yielding her Goodness to these *GREEDY BASTARDS OF THE PHARMACEUTICAL INDUSTRY.*

No Lovey, to my anger, the dirt should turn Lava thus, no one selling anything to Pharmaceutical Greed.

Natural Herbs to combat all our ailments come on now. As humans, we are too dependent on Pharmaceuticals. We should grow all the herbs we need in our backyard to combat every heart issue, lung issue, blood issue, cold issue, vaginal issue, kidney issue, pancreas issue, brain issue, psychological issue, and more.

No man. Enough is enough but then this is to be expected WHEN YOU HAVE DEVILS – DEMONS IN HIGH AND LOW PLACES RUNNING THE GLOBE – EARTH. LIFE – THE LIFE AND RIGHTS OF CITIZENS MATTERS NOT BECAUSE THEY; THESE DEMONS CAN CREATE DISEASES AND VIRUSES AT WILL THAT KILL AND GET AWAY WITH THEIR ATROCITIES.

Now Lovey tell me. WHAT RIGHT DO ANY WHITE PERSON HAVE TO GO INTO BLACK LANDS AND TELL THEM HOW TO LIVE, WHAT TO DO, HOW TO GOVERN THEIR LAND, HOW TO BUILD, HOW TO EAT, WHAT TO EAT, HOW TO RAISE THEIR FAMILY, HOW TO TRULY LIVE AND PRAISE YOU, AND MORE LOVEY?

ARE WE AS BLACKS NOT THE FOOLISH ONES TO KEEP BOWING DOWN TO THE WILL OF DEATH INCLUDING, DEATH'S CHILDREN AND PEOPLE?

So, no. Thank you Lovey. Truly thank you for You and Death because; DEATH PROTECT LIFE BY ENSURING NO ONE WICKED AND EVIL WHO HATH MORE SIN THAN GOOD CAN OR WILL EVER GET ACCESS TO THE REALM AND

WORLD OF LIFE – GOD FROM WHO I CALL LOVEY FROM TIME TO TIME.

To go further. "*TRULY THANK YOU MORE THAN UNCONDITIONALLY LOVEY FOR LOCKING THE WHITE RACE OUT OF LIFE.*"

No Weapon – Evil can, or will ever gain access to your domain. For me now. *IT IS UNFORTUNATE THAT WE CANNOT HAVE THIS MORE THAN FOREVER EVER WITHOUT END LOCK OUT OF THE WHITE RACE NO MATTER GENDER, COLOUR, OR CREED, NATIONALITY HERE ON EARTH AS OF TODAY APRIL 18, 2021, AND EVEN BEFORE THIS DATE IF I CAN CHANGE THE PAST BUT I KNOW I CANNOT.*

NO LOVEY. *PEOPLES LIVES SHOULD NOT COME DOWN TO A FRIGGING VACCINE.*

No Lovey, this *BC RACE NEED TO BE EXTINGUISHED; ERADICATED FROM EARTH.* Yes, harsh but that's the way I feel because; I don't see hell crashing down on them here on Earth despite me seeing *DARKNESS WITH DOTS ABOVE THEM, AND OR, AROUND THEM, AND OR, IN THE SKY ABOVE THEM.*

THEY CANNOT KEEP RUNNING THIS EARTH ON INJUSTICE AND MURDER; DEATH LOVEY COME ON NOW.

WE ARE NOT WHITE THEREFORE, WHY THE BC ARE BLACKS GOVERNING THEIR LAND AND PEOPLE LIKE THEM; DUTTY STINKING WHITE PEOPLE.

No let me lash out reckless and rude at Mother Africa because; SHE IS THE BC CAUSE OF THIS. SHE ALLOWED EVIL INTO HER WORLD AS WELL AS, PROCREATED WITH BC DEATH – EVIL AND DEM LYING AFRICANS HAVE HIDDEN THE TRUTH OF THEM PROCREATING WITH EVIL FROM THE REST OF THE BLACK POPULATION GLOBALLY.

Now let me ask you this truthfully Lovey and be fully, and truly honest with me because; I am pissed to the point where I just want to destroy it all now on Earth to my wrath and anger.

WHEN HAVE AND HAS SO-CALLED BLACK AFRICANS EVER DEFENDED YOU THE BLACK GOD OF LIFE – TRUTH AND TRUE LIFE?

DID THOSE BC BITCHES NOT SELL YOU OUT FI RICE AN PEAS – THE NASTINESS OF BABYLON AND THE

WHITE RACE THUS, YOU HAVE MANY AFRICANS THAT ARE A MIXTURE OF INDIAN AND BLACK AS WELL AS, ALBINO. YES, THE RECESSIVE GENES OF THEIR FRIGGING SIN AND SINS.

No Lovey truly don't stop me. Let me cuss out the ENTIRE AFRICAN KINGDOM OF FILTH.

DEM A DEGENERATE AS FAR AS I AM CONCERNED BECAUSE; THEY KEEP THE LIES OF SIN AND DEATH.

They have no balls or backbone to defend you yet, they claim Black Heritage, and Lineage. Now tell me Lovey. WHAT BLACK HERITAGE, LINEAGE, AND LIFE DO ANY AFRICAN HAVE WITH YOU?

Did many lands – people in Africa not sell you out Lovey thus forfeiting life with you?

Did you not divorce many African Lands and People Lovey because they walked away from you to be BITCHES FOR THE DIFFERENT DEATHS; RACES?

Do they; Africans even know about you, or know you Lovey?

No Lovey. Who the hell are they to call themselves Black when they know not you and or, know you not?

They lie on you.

Are the Tribes of Death period in my view. Therefore, they protect and keep the Lies of Satan. That which Satan's Children and People tell them to do to confuse as well as, **KEEP BLACK NATIONS SHACKLED AND CHAINED TO DEATH LITERALLY.**

So yes, I am truthfully, and honestly **CHALLENGING THE LEGITIMACY OF AFRICA AND AFRICANS FROM THEN UNTIL NOW INCLUDING, TOMORROW LOVEY.**

WHA PAATE A DEM GOOD.

No Lovey, **WHA PAATE A AFRICA GOOD?**

As soon as the Devil came a knocking dem sell out life fi bi **BITCHES – THE BITCHES AND WHORES OF DEATH.** Thus, the colonization of Africa by the different races including, Babylon of Old.

Now let me ask you this Lovey and be fully truthful and honest with me. And Mother Earth stop laughing because you know how deadly my anger can be.

Now Lovey. **AFRICANS CAN TELL THE TRUTH?**

DOES ANY TRUTH LIE IN AFRICA AND AFRICANS?

Oh yes, I went there because I am pissed this morning therefore, I am exercising my rights to be angry and, it is You Lovey I am coming to with my anger because; ALL BLACKS DO NOT COME FROM AFRICA. AND NOT ALL BLACKS SOLD YOU OUT LIKE AFRICANS – BLACK AFRICANS DID.

You Lovey cannot stop the truth because NOT ALL BLACKS ARE BLACKS.

SOME BLACKS ARE WHITE – FALL UNDER THE WHITE BANNER OF DEATH DUE TO SIN; THEIR DYAM "DISOBEDIENCE." THEREFORE, THEY HAVE NO PART AND PARCEL IN LIFE WITH YOU COME ON NOW.

No don't stop me because NOT EVEN DEATH CAN QUELL MY ANGER RIGHT NOW. TRUST ME IF DEATH TRY TO STOP ME, I WILL LITERALLY GO INTO HELL AND BEAT THE CRAP OUT OF DEATH, AND FEMALE BLACK DEATH TO MY ANGER RIGHT NOW, AND TAKE IT ALL FROM THEM.

I am not afraid of Death you know this Lovey come on now.

When the BC are we as Black People going to wake up and take our life back from those that are destroying us literally?

When the BC are they – Blacks going to WAKE THE BLEEP UP AND REALIZE THAT YOU LOVEY DID NOT PUT THE WHITE MAN IN POWER TO OVERSEE ANYONE HERE ON EARTH?

When the BC are they – Blacks going to WAKE THE BLEEP UP AND REALIZE THEIR LIFE HATH WORTH IN LIFE BUT WILL NEVER HAVE WORTH TO DEATH'S CHILDREN AND PEOPLE?

Yes, Death value their life because; IT'S US AS HUMANS THAT GIVE DEATH TIME – LIFE.

No, don't calm me down Lovey before I say something to you that I might live to regret. Let me wain my anger my way. And thank you for not wanting me to get too angry that I SIN RECKLESS AND RUDE WITH MY ANGER. *But Lovey, can we truly not do something here on Earth to* TURN BACK THE ILLS OF THE WHITE RACE ON THEM. LET THEM BE TRULY AFFECTED.

No Lovey, I cannot command Earth, but I do hope Mother Earth feel my anger and see my anger for all the injustice in her, and do something about it by not yielding these evil lands any water or food. Dem dyam wicked let their wickedness feed them literally.

No Lovey. Why can't Black Lands banish Whites from their land as well as, give them absolutely no access to Black Lands?

Why the hell can't we open true, good, and honest trade with all our Black Lands?

"Blacks do not need White Economy." It is Whites that need us for money, our resources, our knowledge, their beating stick, pharmaceutical scapegoats, and guinea pigs, death period.

No Lovey. I am angry and truly forgive me for my anger. You are still my true love in some way despite my words in this book and wanting to divorce you. But with all that said Lovey, you will have Greedy Blacks that will truly sell out their own for a true place in hell literally.

Just as you Lovey can walk away from Blacks, and you did do this; walk away from some Blacks in the Time/Days of Old. You can walk away from all who are wicked and evil here on Earth.

Mother Earth too can do the same thing. Walk away from all who are wicked and evil here on Earth by not yielding her goodness and truth — food and water to any one Wicked and Evil including, the Lands of Evil. And yes, if Mother Earth need me to name these lands, I will not hesitate to do so.

And yes, Jamaica, the United States of America, Israel, Vatican City, Italy, and England, and more are some of these Wicked Lands due to the ills and sins of the people. Remember Lovey, You Lovey deemed Jamaica unclean. Plus, You Lovey have and has forbidden me to go into Jamaica due to the land being unclean — dirty.

Yes, Lovey this is my Vengeance of Anger and, because I am coming to You and Mother Earth directly with my Vengeance of Anger; please forgive me honestly and truthfully.

I know what I don't want for self, I should not want or need for others, but you truly know me when I get angry because Death hath no say when it comes to my Vengeance and Anger.

No Lovey, *I DETEST INJUSTICE POINT BLANK AND PERIOD.*

NO RACE SHOULD HOLD OTHERS BY THE BALLS AND TAKE THEIR LIFE FROM THEM.

And don't You dare say, "and what are you doing with your anger?"

I need justice here on Earth Lovey thus, ABSOLUTELY NO ONE CAN LIVE CLEAN AND TRUE HERE ON EARTH WITH THE WHITE RACE AND RACES OF EVIL AMONGST THEM.

No, this morning we were having such a good time. You, Me, and Mother Earth to the point where I was dreaming about roses. They were so beautiful that the roses could open and close. Yes, this White Man was showing me the roses. Red Roses, aah Pink Roses, and I believe Yellow Roses.

So yes, we have to plant roses Lovey and Mother Earth here on Earth. I have to have my Rose Garden and I know exactly where I want to have it.

I was even telling You and Mother Earth than when I die; well, my flesh dies, I want to be buried in a house. In the house at my head there have to be a waterfall, flowers even if the flowers are artificial in a stand up vase. Yes, I have to have sofa chairs, a bookcase with my books, and yes, we can have a day bed in the house. Plus, the energy that should be around my home to be so powerful that no one can come disturb me with their bullshit. I have to have my impenetrable defences in Death when it comes to evil, and undesirables that feel the need to want to come and disturb my peace. No Lovey, I need the continual energy to keep those people at bay as well as, the power to bax dem dung tu. Do not disturb my resting place period.

This is not Egypt where you have GRAVE ROBBERS robbing the dead and disturbing their resting place. GRAVE ROBBERS whose descent are not Black. Thus, Babylon did invade Egypt and robbed Black Egyptians of their Birthright. Now, they claim Egypt as their own. But Lovey. Not in my WORLD AND LIFE WITH YOU AND OUR GOOD AND TRUE OWN. Impenetrable frames, frameworks, and foundations we must have continually without end from undesirables; all who are not of life period.

No Lovey. BAX DUNG wicked and rude if undesirables disturb our resting place.

FLATTA DEM period. Let me rest.

Mother Earth was showing me that another Volcano is going to erupt but I truly do not know where. So yes, EARTH IS GOING TO BURN LITERALLY.

Man worried about their damned vaccine yet know not the STARVATION AND LACK OF CLEAN DRINKING WATER THAT IS GOING TO BE ON EARTH.

No Lovey, You and Mother Earth will not save the Wicked and Evil of Earth period. I am forbidding the both of you to because;

I WILL SAVE NONE IF I AM THE SAVING GRACE OF HUMANITY.

I more than honestly and truthfully including, categorically will not save anyone wicked and evil period.

No Lovey, **the NERVE OF HIM TRYING TO FIND ME IN DEATH. BITCH STAY THE HELL IN HELL. YOU SHOULD HAVE KNOWN THE CONSEQUENCES OF MARRYING INTO THAT SINFUL AND DECEITFUL DEMONIC FAMILY.**

PP of the English Monarch coming to me. Bitch burn. I will forever ever shut your ass down. Don't find me thus, my prayer to God and Mother Earth to shut you the hell down from ever finding me.

I know the hell of England and their Monarch. Bitch, **THE BIBLE OF MAN THAT WAS COMMISSIONED BY KING JAMES WAS TRULY NOT CALLED FOR.**

HOW MANY HAVE AND HAS DIED BECAUSE OF DEATH'S BOOK.

HOW MANY ARE DEAD TO GOD RIGHT NOW BECAUSE OF DEATH'S BOOK: KING JAMES BIBLE?

HOW MANY HAS AND HAVE FORFEITED LIFE BECAUSE OF DEATH'S BOOK – KING JAMES BIBLE?

Bleep Off. THE LOTS OF YOU ARE DEAD. THE CHILDREN AND PEOPLE OF DEATH SO KISS MY NATURAL BROWN ASS – YES, BLACK ASS BECAUSE I WILL NEVER EVER SAVE YOU OR SAVE ANY IN YOUR FAMILY.

Remember this:

LOVEY - GOD.

England discredited my Black God for whom I call Lovey.

England took hundreds of millions if not billions of Blacks from Lovey.

Do you think I would forgive any of you for what you did to Lovey, Black People, Scotland?

No, calm Michelle, calm. Calm your temper. If you go off more, Hell would sure to come down and devour the Earth right away because; you would have pissed off Death to wrath.

Calm your temper Michelle.
Calm your temper.

Think of Lovey, You, Mother Earth, and your true love of Water Spouts, and its beauty.

Calm you Michelle.

Dyam bright.

No Lovey, im dyam bright.

Lovey, yu a mi bunnununus, and dis dutty drangcrow a fine mi.

Cuya man. Si di demons of hell dey. Go do wey Jamaicans wi tell yu fi du tu yu maada.

Dooone fine mi eva again. Mi an yu anno fren.

No Lovey. People truly do not think of their sins, the sins of their ancestors; forefathers and mothers, their children, parents, friends, the people they rape and kill, the lies they tell on You Lovey, the ills they do to Mother Earth, and More.

Sins stick.
Sins accumulate.
Sins take you from life.

Sins get you locked out of Life; the World and Realm of God – Lovey.

Sins kill.
Sins destroy.
Sins take you to hell.
Sins defy life.
Sins are abominations, and more.

LIES TOLD ON GOD ONLY GOD CAN FORGIVE. THUS, THE WHITE RACE HAS AND HAVE TOLD LIES ON GOD, DESTROYED LIVES HERE ON EARTH, KILLED, HAVE AND HAS DONE ALL TO KILL EARTH AND ALL

LIFE. NOW, IN DEATH SOME OF YOU ARE WANTING SAVING FROM HELL AFTER FINDING OUT THE AMOUNT OF TIME YOU HAVE TO SPEND IN HELL BURNING.

Bitch don't look at me or find me because, I am not as generous as God and Mother Earth. I am not that forgiving especially when it comes to God and Mother Earth period.

Bitch do you think Death would let you go?

Death is literally smiling at you right now. You were a sacrifice. All who marry into that Demonic Family **are a sacrifice – offering unto death.** *You should have known that. Well, you just found out if you did not know.*

Many of you think you know. Bitch I can tell you all about hell.

Can tell you how hell work.
Can tell you of the fire that burn your spirit.

Shit, I know Death – the different Deaths of Humans – the Different Races.

AS FOR YOU THE CORRUPT BLACK LEADERS OF THE GLOBE, I WOULD GET A COPY OF THE NEW BOOK OF KNOWLEDGE as written by Michelle and Lovey – God real soon because, wow to the Death Penalty I added unto your asses. Sin Penalty

True Blacks are not White therefore, you cannot live corrupt and mistreat your Black Own. Therefore, truly woe be unto the lots of you.

YOU DO NOT LIVE TO KILL. YOU LIVE TO LIVE.

YOU DO NOT LIVE TO BE UNJUST. YOU LIVE JUST, CLEAN, HONEST, AND TRUE.

YOU DO NOT LIVE TO TELL LIES. YOU LIVE TO TELL THE TRUTH SO THAT GOD WILL FIND FAVOUR IN YOU AND SAVE YOU FROM THE CONFINES OF HELL – DEATH.

THE LIES KING JAMES COMMISSIONED TO BE WRITTEN WAS NOT CALLED FOR. HE LIED ON GOD THUS, SACRIFICING BILLIONS TO DEATH HERE ON EARTH WITH DEATH'S BOOK. SO-CALLED HOLY BIBLE THAT HAS HIS NAME ON IT.

BITCH THE ENGLISH MONARCH LIED ON GOD AND USED THE BIBLE OF MAN AS A WEAPON TO GO OUT THERE TO ROB, RAPE, STEAL, MURDER; TAKE HUMANS FROM LIFE. You didn't think the SINS OF ENGLAND AND THE BRITISH MONARCH FROM THEN UNTIL THE TIME OF YOUR PASSING WOULDN'T FALL ON YOU?

<u>EVERY INDIVIDUAL THAT IS A BRITISH CITIZEN NO MATTER WHERE IN THE GLOBLE THEY ARE IN HAVE AND HAS INHERITED THE SIN AND SINS OF THE BRITSH MONARCH.</u> *Well expect for my family – those who are dare and true to me.*

People pick up a copy of <u>**THE NEW BOOK OF KNOWLEDGE.**</u> *There are two books. And yes, I am pushing these books for you to see and know the penalty associated with one sin.*

Do not squawk at me pushing and or, telling you to pick up a copy of these books. <u>**YOU NEED TO BE IN THE KNOW.**</u>

You have a life here on Earth. Therefore, ensure while here on Earth your <u>**GOOD OUTWEIGH YOUR SINS.**</u>

I cannot re-iterate anymore.

<u>'THE LIFE YOU LIVE HERE ON EARTH DETERMINES WHERE YOU GO AFTER THE SPIRIT SHED THE FLESH."</u>

I cannot re-iterate anymore.

<u>"GOD CANNOT FORGIVE YOU OF SINS – YOUR SINS DONE UNTO OTHERS."</u> *It's the person you wronged – erred that must forgive you. So, if you wronged John Brown, and John Brown died without forgiving you, then that sin – wrong done to John Brown remains on your*

Sin Record. Therefore, *you need to know the PENALTY OF 1 SIN, AND THE REWARD OF 1 GOOD.*

Now onwards I go with this book.

Look how many Black Lands Globally England – European Whites have conquered.

Look how many Blacks were raped and killed in the name of Greed; your; their greed and Death.

Hell no. *THERE IS NO MERCY HERE FOR THE BLEEPING MERCILESS.* And when I say bleeping everyone use the f word because bleeping is my substitution of the f word.

No Lovey, I don't want to get into my dream with Rawpa Crawpa. Him talking about how beautiful I believe the big girl and or, woman is, him saying we are pretty women, and I said something, and he said no the other one. The other one being Pretty Woman by Julia Roberts and he began to sing the song Pretty Woman. Him walking towards me singing the song. He was dressed in a reddish and or, burgundy leather outfit. After singing his song, he went under way and he fell down and hit his head I believe, and I asked him if he was okay.

See in the dream Rawpa Crawpa reminded me of my ex-husband. Therefore, I told you the entire dream because in the dream it seemed as if Rawpa Crawpa was here in Canada.

Do hope Rawpa Crawpa will be okay. As for my ex-husband, I will not worry about him. There is no love lost there period.

As for my Aunt, I have to worry about her because; Death is coming her way. Yes, more Death is coming in my family on both *sides. But I cannot stop death in this way because, it was ordained. Even I am going to die because I could feel Death when I was telling Mother Earth, and God about my final internment – resting place.*

I believe there were more dreams, but I cannot tell you them because I so can't remember them.

Listen everyone. **RELIGION IS NO DIFFERENT FROM POLITICS. They both kill.**

Your life is worth it therefore, live right and true; honest here on Earth because, I told you in other books and this one.

"THE LIFE YOU LIVE HERE ON EARTH DETERMINES WHERE YOU GO ONCE THE SPIRIT SHED THE FLESH."

I've also told you in other books and this one.

"GOD CANNOT FORGIVE YOU OF YOUR SINS DONE ONTO OTHERS. GOD CAN ONLY FORGIVE YOU OF SINS DONE UNTO GOD."

So, if you wronged and or, erred Mr. Wright down the road. It is Mr. Wright to forgive you. Meaning, if you go to Mr. Wright and say, "Mr. Wright please forgive me for cussing you out reckless and rude because I stole your goat." If Mr. Wright forgives you for stealing his goat and cussing him Mr. Wright out, then that sin have to be; must be removed from your Sin Record – Debt with Death because, Mr. Wright did forgive you. Death must also record the date and time you were forgiven.

And yes, Mr. Wright can ask you for a Sin Offering in return. Mr. Wright can ask you for the cost – sale price of the goat you stole from him as well as, Mental Distress for cussing him out.

So, know <u>*FOR A FACT WITHOUT DOUBT.*</u>

<u>*GOD CANNOT FORGIVE YOU OF SINS DONE UNTO TO OTHERS. IF GOD DID THIS; FORGIVE YOU OF SINS DONE UNTO OTHERS, THEN GOD WOULD BE SINNING AND, GOD CANNOT SIN FOR MAN; ANYONE.*</u>

Yes, not even me.

And yes, my temper is waned for now.

So yes, this is part in part why <u>**BLACKS ARE SUFFERING GLOBALLY. GOD HAS NOT FORGIVEN MANY OF OUR ANCESTORS FOR THE LIES THEY ACCEPTED THUS, ABANDONING GOD; GOOD AND TRUE LIFE.**</u> *As Blacks, we too are guilty. Therefore, we should not complain if God truly do not answer many of us because:* <u>**THE DIVORCE BY GOD WAS INDEFINITE.**</u>

Nothing some of us do will change God's heart because; <u>**AS A RACE AND PEOPLE, WE DID HURT GOD.**</u>

<u>*People, we left God for ALL THAT IS UNCLEAN.*</u> *Now look at us.* <u>**LIKE DOGS BEGGING FOR A BONE FROM GOD.**</u>

WHY THE HELL SHOULD GOD SAVE US WHEN UNTIL NOW WE CANNOT FULLY AND TRUTHFULLY GO TO GOD IN TRUTH AND SAY; GOD TRULY FORGIVE ME FOR HURTING YOU, AND CONDEMNING LIFE.

TRULY FORGIVE ME FOR CHOOSING DEATH OVER YOU. I WANT NOT DEATH ANYMORE, I NEED LIFE; YOU SO TRULY FORGIVE ME.

Please allow me to amend my ways with you.

I know I've cause you pain. Truly forgive me because I did not know the truth until now. Yes, many things I fully and truly don't know but for hurting you, truly forgive me. Help me to help me come back to you truthfully, and clean. Your Name whether it be John, Michelle, Stephen, Steven, Lyle, and so forth. But you get the idea.

But not many of us as Blacks can do this. Many of you will defend religion and the god and gods you're given to take you from life.

Many of you cannot see nor want to know the truth.

Just as we are lied to about our History, Beginning, Contribution to Life; Creation, we are lied to about God – our God of Truth and Life. Therefore, God has and have been made out to be nasty.

Many truly do not know that Religion is not Black or African.

Many refuse to accept the Truth of Life therefore, many Blacks refuse their own Black God thus, hundreds of millions if not billions of Blacks are living wrong; for Death.

Therefore, many cannot be the better person and go to God for truth and true forgiveness. All that the Children and People of Death offers is too lucrative here on Earth so why the hell should God save any of you from the HELL YOU CREATED FOR SELF HERE ON EARTH?

And don't you dare say; "well God don't answer you all the time thus this book and book one."

Certain things God need not answer me for because I know the answer to them.

Listen, I like bugging God. Well, TRULY LOVE BUGGING GOD BECAUSE I AM SPOILT. THERE ARE DAYS WHEN I NEED GOD TO LITERALLY SPOIL ME MY WAY. Plus, I know that GOD CANNOT GIVE WHAT HE CANNOT GIVE.

And don't go there about me not having a man and or, companion, and my loneliness at times. I recently met someone, but I've prayed to God not to let it pan out. He's not what I want and need in life right now therefore, I truly do not need a relationship with him. We can be friends but nothing else. I see, and I am not one for darkness. Never mind. Just let it go because I need to keep God not chase God and Mother Earth away. Hey, Mama; I need to see my Water Spout, and hold that beautiful Water Spout in my hand.

And none of you better come and say, I am racist, I have no merit in life, God should throw me out, God should leave me alone and abandon me, death should have their way with me; all the negatives please do not throw back at me because it will come back to haunt you in a harsh and bitter way. You will die. There are no ands, ifs, or buts about this.

God and life is not a toy or a, play thing.

Think.

THE TRUTH CANNOT LIE FOR YOU.

You do not like what is written in this book. Well put yourself in the shoe of others if you can.

Now tell me. <u>For all the ills – murders you in the White Race has and have committed over the years and centuries; do any of you think you can compensate the families for the lives you've taken from them?</u>

All the lies your Race: White Race have and has told on God, Earth, Outer Space, Black People as well as, other Races; do you in the White Race think you can compensate any?

Lies are Sins and you the White race <u>STAND AS THE UNFORGIVEN RACE.</u> Thus, God did lock you out of Life. Now tell me. Where are the lots of you going to go apart from hell?

Is all that is happening here on Earth necessary?
Are the lies that are told day in and day out necessary?

Was Covid-19 and all the diseases and viruses that are made in laboratories by the wicked and evil to infect and kill others necessary?

Who is being held PRISONERS TO PHARMACEUTICAL GREED?

Who are the test subjects for PHARMACEUTICAL GREED?

Did God commission all the ills of Earth to happen?

Are we as humans not the ones to PROCREATE WITH EVIL PEOPLE AND BRING FORTH EVIL PEOPLE THAT LIVE TO DESTROY AND KILL?

IS IT NOT HUMANS DESTROYING AND KILLING EARTH?

IS IT, AND WAS IT NOT HUMANS THAT HAS AND HAVE STOPPED THE GROWTH – EXPANSION OF EARTH; MOTHER EARTH WITH OUR SINS – EVILS WE DO DAY IN AND DAY OUT?

So, none of you don't come to me with the RACIST CARD *because; all you have to do is;* GO TO GOD IN PRAYER AND OR, TRUTH; TRUE TALK FOR THE TRUTH.

Further, the Racist Card is thrown around day in and day out like people changing their underwear.

Know this and learn this.

"I DON'T HAVE TO LIKE YOU OR HIRE YOU."

It is my God Given Right not to like you for the evils you do day in and day out. Your colour matters not to me. Therefore, I refuse to spread hate even when I get racist. My life with God is worth it therefore, I petition God and Mother Earth for the Good and True Only. Yes, to keep us safe, fed, away from all who are wicked and evil, and more. So, truly don't come to me, or at me with your Racist Card. I will cuss you out and school you.

Hate is truly not me, it's you. You want and need to justify you and your views. I refuse to spread hate or tell anyone to hate.

Hate is Death and I have absolutely not time to hate your ass. Why the hell should I hate and add Sin to my Sin Record?

Bitch you're not worth it.
Know this:

"ABSOLUTELY NO ONE CAN TAKE COLOUR OF SKIN TO GOD TO GAIN ACCESS TO THE WORLD AND REALM OF GOD."

Listen, God did not, nor do God put dirty people to oversee anyone. God would not be that vile and wicked - evil.

Now look into yourself, your religious beliefs, your life, and tell me
if <u>YOU ARE LIVING FOR LIFE – GOD AND YOURSELF OR, ARE YOU LIVING FOR DEATH; A PLACE AND LIFE WITH DEATH IN HELL?</u>

Good and true life cannot be biased, one sided, unjust, unbalanced; wrong. God and true life have to be; must be true, honest, right, clean, positive, ever growing, and more good and true things.

<u>Life – God cannot live to please you and your beliefs of what you think is right and what you think is wrong.</u>

<u>Ills are not from God. Ills are from Man; us as a people; race and people; humans.</u>

Music:
<u>IT'S RAINING RIDDIM MIX</u> – *Brickwell Label*

Listen, <u>CHEMISTRY **by Sanchez**</u> *remind(s) me of how we as humans lie on God, do all that is wicked and evil to God and Mother Earth then expect God to save us just like that.*

<u>DON'T CRY **by Daddy Screw;**</u> *I would like to dedicate truthfully, honestly, and clean to Mother Earth. You are the Sustainer and Maintainer of Humans here on Earth, and all humans have and has done is use and abuse you day in and day out.*

It's time now as Mother to take your goodness from all who abuse you. People like; Pharmaceutical Greed; Corporate Owners,

Farmers who plant with chemicals, Politicians who use your land – earth as their dumping ground for weapons, nuclear weapons, war, and more.

Therefore, find a common ground with God and get your Visa and Passport and leave humans to their own demise. You're not the Bitch of Humans therefore, truly save yourself.

Rejoin good and true with God. Squash all that has and have separated the both of you, and let go of all who are wicked and evil no matter the energy and form of all that/who are wicked and evil.

Michelle

I so don't want to end this book but I am going to have to.

It's April 19, 2021 and things are different for me in some way. I feel as if there is greatness to come for me despite my death. I will not expect you to comprehend the __"despite my death."__

I am at peace and this is great and good for me. At any rate, my dreams wow.

Like I said in another book. My mind truly do not work on the same level as many of you. Therefore, I am going to ask this.

__With all the Ash from the Volcano in St. Vincent; I was wondering, can the people not use the Ash for Cosmetics. Instead of letting and or, storing the Ash by the Wayside. Find a way to use it for Cosmetics; face masks; mud mask that clean your pores including, Ash Baths?__

With the weight of the Ash, can the Ash not be incorporated and or, be amalgamated with Cement, and used as Stucco for homes.

To me, it would be a waste to let all that Ash go to waste.

Hey, my thinking is different.

As for Brazil, I truly do not know what is happening in that land when it comes to fruits. Dreamt I was walking on the sidewalk and fruit trees were on people's property. Raspberries, Strawberries, Guava. When you think Guava think Taiwanese Guava.

There was a lot of fruits on the trees, but the fruits were spoiling; were rotten. I could not get fresh organic fruits. There were also these ladies walking and they went on this woman's property and they were talking about her plant; tree. Continuing to walk, I picked a Guava and on the Guava, it had a Brazil Label on it and I thought it weird. Then the labelling disappeared.

Like I said, I do not know what is going on in Brazil, nor do I know what is going to happen there, food wise when it comes to fruits and vegetables. So, something is truly not right food and or, fruit wise in South America and, I would go as far as saying Asian Lands including, China.

I will leave South America, and Asia alone because; I know many lands are going to feel it water and food wise shortly.

Am I being guided on the right path by Mother Earth right now?

Yes, and I have to follow this path because this is the right and true path for me.

I did have other dreams and it had to do with me and this child; Female Black Child and my son. The child was clinging to me. Therefore, I do hope positive changes come my way family wise where I find my space and truly live the way I need to live good and true.

Will tell you all about it when it happens. In the meantime, stay safe, focused, blessed, good and true, healthy, wise, financially stable, and more good things despite the happenings here on Earth.

Michelle

BOOKS WRITTEN BY MICHELLE JEAN 2021

MY TALK JANUARY 2021

MY TALK JANUARY 2021 – BOOK TWO

MINI BOOK

JUST TALKING – THINKING

A LITTLE TALK WITH MOTHER EARTH

I NEED ANSWERS GOD

POETRY MY WAY

THE MIND AND SPIRITUALITY

COMING SOON

MY NIGHTS